# SOCIETY IN
# VOGUE

'Elfine obediently resumed her reading aloud of *Our Lives From Day to Day*, from an April number of *Vogue* . . .

'"I don't like *Our Lives* very much, Flora. It's all rather in a hurry, isn't it, and wanting to tell you how nice it was?"

'"I do not propose that you shall found a life-philosophy upon *Our Lives From Day to Day*, Elfine. I merely make you read it because you will have to meet people who do that kind of thing . . ."'

From *Cold Comfort Farm*
by Stella Gibbons 1932

# SOCIETY IN
# VOGUE

**THE INTERNATIONAL SET
BETWEEN THE WARS**

CONDÉ NAST BOOKS
London Sydney Auckland Johannesburg

First published in 1992 by Condé Nast Publications Ltd,
an imprint of Random House UK Ltd, Random House,
20 Vauxhall Bridge Road, London SW1V 2SA

Random House Australia (Pty) Ltd, 20 Alfred Street,
Milsons Point, Sydney, New South Wales 2061, Australia

Random Century New Zealand Ltd, 18 Poland Road,
Glenfield, Auckland 10, New Zealand

Random Century South Africa (Pty) Ltd, PO Box 337,
Bergvlei 2012, South Africa

Edited by Cindy Richards
Designed by Polly Dawes

Set in Bauer Bodoni by
SX Composing Ltd, Rayleigh, Essex
Printed and bound in Great Britain
by Butler and Tanner Ltd, Frome and London

A catalogue record for this book is
available from the British Library

ISBN 0 09 177169 2

# CONTENTS

In March 1942, as the dangers and hardships of the
Second World War mounted, an editorial in *Vogue*
magazine showed a pile of Cecil Beaton's society
portraits, lying as if discarded on a studio floor.
'These photographs of great ladies, of great beauties, of
fashion and fashionables, were taken for *Vogue*', ran the
text; 'they have been published in *Vogue*; they are of the
essence of *Vogue*.' Now, to support the war-effort, they
were being sent for pulp, to be recycled as 'packets for food
stuffs', or 'wrappings for machine parts'. It was a telling
image. For two decades – ever since the ending of the previous war, in 1918 – such photographs had epitomised the
world of *Vogue*. Issue by issue, readers had followed the
glamorous lives of these American hostesses, British aristocrats and French elegantes, as they sunbathed on the
Riviera, skiied in St Moritz, entertained in Palm Beach or
presented their debutante daughters at Buckingham
Palace. Now that way of life had gone for ever. Women who
once posed in couture dresses for photographers were
working for the war-effort in uniforms and Utility suits;
artifice had given way to reality; and Cecil Beaton's
elaborate portraits were 'a treasure-trove for the wastepaper collector'. It was the end of an era – for society and
for *Vogue*.

When *Vogue* first appeared, in 1892, it was a small, illus-
trated, weekly gazette, produced in New York for a limited
– but distinguished – readership. Described by the publish-
ers as 'a dignified authentic journal of society, fashion and
the ceremonial side of life', the new magazine had the back-
ing of some of America's most prominent society figures,
from the Astors and the Whitneys to Cornelius Vanderbilt
and Mrs Stuyvesant Fish; and throughout the 1890s it reflected their tastes, in an elegant editorial mixture of
fashion reports, arts reviews, social news and humorous
features. By the early years of the twentieth century, however, the original publishing team had dispersed, and
*Vogue*'s appeal was flagging. In 1909 it was sold; and on the
contents page for the 24 June issue (which included such
features as 'Poultry Raising for Profit and Pleasure') an unfamiliar name appeared for the first time as president –
Condé Nast. A mid-Westerner, of French and German
descent, Nast had not been born into society; but he was an

'The stuff of
Vogue'
BEATON 1942

ambitious, successful publisher of exceptional sophistication and taste, and he understood the requirements of a fashionable readership. Under Nast's direction it was announced that 'a bigger, a better and a still more attractive *Vogue*' was to be published fortnightly; and in the months that followed his take-over, the little social journal began to be transformed into one of the most famous and influential women's magazines of the twentieth century.

*Vogue's* social cachet was to be the key to its success. While other women's magazines competed for mass-circulation sales, it was *Vogue's* 'avowed mission', in Condé Nast's words, to appeal 'not merely to women of great wealth, but more fundamentally, to women of taste'. Where such an elite readership could be assured, high advertising revenues would follow. By early 1911, Nast's commitment to quality and 'class' had been rewarded. Every name on the New York Social Register was claimed to be a subscriber – and Nast announced boldly that '*Vogue* . . . dominates its field as does no other publication.' Already, *Vogue* was beginning to develop a mystique which it would never lose.

For women of taste, wealth and leisure, and those with aspirations, the magazine became required reading. Beautifully presented, and filled with fine quality black-and-white photographs, the early issues of *Vogue* contained an unrivalled blend of society news and comment; reports from the smart resorts and sophisticated foreign capitals; features on theatres, books and music – and, most important, authoritative fashion reporting. In an era when fashion and society were still virtually inseparable, what Paris decreed, and what the smart world wore – at every event, from the Opera to horse-shows – were subjects of the highest interest to the readers at whom *Vogue* was directed. When, in the late autumn of 1914, *Vogue* sponsored a war-charity fashion gala (the first of its kind), the doyenne of American etiquette, Emily Post, wrote approvingly, 'It was an extraordinary achievement . . . for Fashion, meaning clothes, and Fashion, meaning the smart world, were represented, as they should be, together.' For three decades, *Vogue's* editorial formula was to be based on that glamorous combination.

The Great War of 1914-18 served, ironically, to assist,

Mrs Stuyvesant
Fish
1913

'A stimulus to recruitment': two popular New York bachelors, Captain Maurice Burke Roche and Ensign Francis Burke Roche. The elder twin, in 1920, inherited the British title Baron Fermoy – and was the grandfather of the present Princess of Wales
WHITE STUDIO 1918

rather than hinder, *Vogue*'s progress. In Britain as well as in America, a readership either ignorant of the horrors unfolding in Europe, or seeking distraction from such knowledge, continued to demand its fortnightly copies of *Vogue* – which still, behind colourful patriotic covers, offered enticing features on furs and jewels, notes on sports and holidays, and advertisements for luxury cars, along with news of society women's war-work, and photographs of popular New York bachelors in uniform. When *Vogue* could no longer be exported to Britain, because of Atlantic shipping losses, Condé Nast turned the potential setback into a step forward – by launching, in 1916, a separate British edition of the magazine. It was to prove a highly advantageous move. There were now two *Vogue*s, each with its own national style and readership, but working in close alliance, and constantly exchanging photographs, articles and illustrations, so that much of the best material appeared in both. (After 1921, when French *Vogue* was launched, there would be three editions.) As the First World War drew to its end, and the restless, effervescent 1920s dawned, *Vogue* was ideally placed to reflect the new world of international society, as it 'jazzed' and gossiped, entertained and shopped – ever on the move, always in pursuit of new forms of stimulation and amusement. 'Le Monde Qui S'Amuse', a favourite phrase of the *Vogue* columnists, had never seemed so apt a description of the smart world.

'The old days are here again', *Vogue* declared in the aftermath of the Armistice; but for once the magazine was mistaken. The old days had gone for good, and the war had altered everything: from clothes and manners, art and ideas, to social attitudes. Dorothy Parker, an American *Vogue* staff journalist, wrote with her usual perception in 1919, 'The style in heroines has changed completely. In fact, the style in all women has changed.' *Vogue*'s heroines were no longer the stately, corseted grandes dames of pre-war New York and London, such as Mrs Stuyvesant Fish, but slender, boyish, youthful creatures, who drove their own cars, powdered their noses in public, and shocked the old guard with their bobbed hair and short skirts. Princess Marthe Bibesco, writing in *Vogue* a few years later, recalled with approval how Chanel revolutionised fashion in the early 1920s by putting rich and aristocratic women into brief, simple, jersey dresses and necklaces of glass beads – 'the uniform of the poor'. Debutantes smoked, kissed their men-friends in public and danced the Charleston opposite their partners, instead of waltzing conventionally in their arms; fashionable speech acquired a dizzy absurdity. ('Tinketty-most-frightfully-tonk, old tin of fruit! . . . what price a couple of cocktails at the Ritz?' mimicked British *Vogue* in 1923.) Progress and modernity were the watchwords now; and by the mid-1920s even the most hidebound were beginning to adapt their ideas. 'Queen Mary, who formerly looked upon even the old one-step with disapproval, now smiles serenely if she meets a "jazz" band', wrote *Vogue* in 1924, adding, 'There are gentlemen jockeys, lady air-pilots, titled crooks . . . A decade has changed the world.'

'She actually
powders her nose
in public'
FISH 1919

Douglas Fairbanks
Jr 'shooting' at
Shawford
1937

Noel Coward in
his 'futurist flat'
1927

Society was no longer so easily defined and contained as in former days. 'The world is growing smaller, the gates of Society wider,' declared American *Vogue*. 'All the stuffy, musty Victorian fetishes about birth are being cast aside.' Even in Britain, where old snobberies died hard, notions of social acceptability changed radically. *Vogue*'s gossip column, 'How One Lives From Day to Day', (also called 'Our Lives From Day to Day') increasingly mentioned names from the world of showbusiness – American entertainers and film-stars, British theatricals – alongside those of aristocrats and fashionable hostesses. At Condé Nast's legendary parties in his Park Avenue penthouse (decorated by Elsie de Wolfe), the guests might range from Mrs William Randolph Hearst, Princess Nathalie Paley and the Astors to Cary Grant and Groucho Marx; at dinner Mrs Cornelius Vanderbilt might be seated next to Jascha Heifetz, or George Gershwin. Photographs taken at English country house-parties showed Douglas Fairbanks Junior staying with Lady Morvyth Benson's family at Shawford Park, and Tallulah Bankhead at historic Wilton – while the glamorous, witty presence of Noel Coward, who was born in suburban Teddington, set the seal of success on the chicest London and New York gatherings. By the same process, those born into society began to explore the possibilities of areas once thought of as taboo, from shop-keeping to advertising. Decorating (where Elsie de Wolfe had boldly led the way, since before the War) now became an ultrafashionable profession for society women; noblemen's daughters appeared on the stage; and some of Britain's most aristocratic beauties, including Viscountess Curzon and Lady Louis Mountbatten, appeared in advertisements for Pond's Cold Cream. 'Anything Goes!' sang Cole Porter, with truth.

The new social cocktail required skilful mixing, however. Under the editorship of the mannish, intellectual Dorothy Todd, in the early 1920s, British *Vogue* began – in the opinion of Condé Nast and American *Vogue*'s editor, Edna Woolman Chase – to lean too heavily towards the arty and Bohemian aspects of English upper-class life. The novelist Aldous Huxley joined the staff, bringing with him his Bloomsbury Group friends. Virginia Woolf and David Garnett contributed book reviews, articles and short stories;

Clive Bell became *Vogue*'s art-critic; and even the decoration features reflected Bloomsbury tastes, with photographs of the Hon Vita Sackville-West's country house, and the economist Maynard Keynes's Cambridge University rooms, decorated by Vanessa Bell and Duncan Grant. The results were brilliant – but not necessarily what readers seeking details of Lelong dresses and winter sports parties expected to find in *Vogue*. After Miss Todd's departure, the editorial tone lightened once more – and by the late 1920s there was a new spirit of gaiety and wit abroad, as the name 'Cecil Beaton' began to appear with increasing frequency in the magazine.

Beaton was to be one of society's most indefatigable chroniclers, as well as one of the twentieth century's most important photographers. It was as an artist, rather than a photographer, that he began his career with *Vogue* in 1927, drawing witty, sketchy (but always flattering) little cartoons of society figures such as Lady Diana Cooper and Mrs Sacheverell Sitwell, under the heading 'Portraits in Passing'. Beaton's caricatures of the smart world proved popular with both British and American readers, and soon he was writing articles on such topics as 'The Fun of Dressing-Up', contributing to the 'How One Lives . . . ' column, and taking blurry, but imaginative portraits, against boldly stylised backgrounds. His first visit to New York, in 1928, marked a turning-point: Condé Nast gave him a handsome contract (while insisting that he improve the quality of his photography, to meet *Vogue*'s inexorably high standards) and the doors of American society opened to him. 'The fabulousness, the kindness, the brightness . . . the smartness!' Beaton marvelled to his American *Vogue* readers. Everyone of note, from the Harrison Williamses, the Alfred Lunts and Anita Loos, to Fred Astaire and his fascinating sister Adèle, seemed now to be among his friends (and sitters). While *Vogue* represented all that Beaton most enjoyed, such as beauty, fashion, the theatre, society, he in turn was 'everything *Vogue* wanted . . . the perfect balance of Inside *Vogue* and Outside World.' At a time when fashion and society were truly international, he moved effortlessly between Britain, America and France, reporting from Hollywood and Monte Carlo, Palm Beach and Baden-Baden, the Venice Lido and St Moritz. In his work

Fred Astaire with his sister and dancing-partner Adèle (later Lady Charles Cavendish) STEICHEN 1927

*Above* Lady Diana
Cooper models a
hat for Vogue
NICKOLAS MURAY
1924

*Below* Mrs Freda
Dudley Ward
HOWARD AND JOAN
COSTER 1928

for *Vogue* during the 1920s and 1930s, Beaton was to create enduring images of an age.

It was *Vogue*'s job to know everything that was happening, and be a step ahead – in the realms of fashion and society alike. Everything about the magazine had to exude quality and a sophisticated authority, from the clothes on the fashion pages, to the grand houses in the decorating features. Lady Diana Cooper and Lady Abdy were invited to model hats for *Vogue*; Lady Louis Mountbatten, Charles de Beistegui and Mrs Paris Singer allowed their apartments in Park Lane, Paris and Palm Beach to be shown in the magazine. The emphasis was on the latest, and the best. *Vogue*'s photographers included Steichen and Man Ray, Hoyningen-Heuné and Horst; the illustrations were by Carl Erickson, Vertès, Christian Bérard; the writers included Nancy Mitford, Colette and Noel Coward. Even the advertisements, for Cartier, Cunard Lines, Rolls-Royce, were redolent of luxury and taste. Everything in *Vogue*'s world had to be presented with an idealised face. Photographs of stout society matrons would be re-touched – 'Slice the hips, that sag must *go*!' Beaton would exclaim – and parties and people were invariably described in flattering terms, 'gay', 'amusing', 'charming' and 'popular' becoming the most overworked of adjectives. Any editorial criticism was reserved for the pretentious and socially inept – such as overbearing (unnamed) charity hostesses, and (anonymous) debutantes who fluttered about the grouse-moors in unsuitable shoes.

In an era and milieu fizzing with every kind of vice and folly, from adultery and drug-use to blackmail, scandal was carefully excluded from *Vogue*'s social columns. The uninitiated reader in Lyme Regis, or Little Rock, would not have learned from *Vogue* which leading members of society were active homosexuals and lesbians – even if Miss Elsa Maxwell's Eton crop and tendency to appear as President Hoover, or General Hindenberg, at fancy-dress balls caused some to wonder. The troubled, much-married Barbara Hutton was described with unqualified admiration in terms of her 'exquisite, dazzling beauty', and 'fabulous jewels'; while references to the chic Mrs Freda Dudley Ward, and Thelma, Lady Furness, gave away no hint of their intimate relationships with the Prince of Wales.

Though probably better-informed than any other publication where royal amours were concerned, *Vogue* maintained an absolute, high-bred discretion on the subject. Long after the handsome, popular Prince, heir to the British throne and Empire, had become deeply involved with the twice-married American divorcée Wallis Simpson, for whom he would eventually abdicate, *Vogue* betrayed no hint of what was afoot – except to those able to read between the lines. It was part of a growing relationship between the future Duchess of Windsor and the magazine which would ultimately pay publishing dividends.

Mrs Ernest Simpson had first appeared in the pages of *Vogue* at the end of the 1920s, when she arrived in London with her second husband, and began to establish herself as a hostess of considerable charm and taste. She was photographed for the magazine by Man Ray, in an 'outfit of great simplicity and elegance', and thereafter her name cropped up from time to time in the 'Our Lives From Day to Day' column. In the early 1930s, the tone of such references subtly changed. Mrs Simpson would be mentioned, carefully separated by several lines, in the same paragraph as the Prince of Wales. Her ideas for cocktail snacks were quoted in a 1935 feature on entertaining, with disconcerting deference ('Of course, it would be Mrs Ernest Simpson who first thought up the wonderful combination of seeded white grapes with little cubes of Dutch cheese, stuck through with a wooden cocktail stick') and a Beaton photograph of her, in a grave and gracious pose, appeared in American *Vogue* in that year. By the beginning of 1937, the Prince had become King Edward VIII, and the royal love-affair was out in the open. American readers, understandably, were avid for pictures of Mrs Simpson, and *Vogue* was able to oblige with two pastel drawings, for which she sat to Cecil Beaton, and an intriguing pen-portrait. ('Of late her general appearance has become infinitely more distinguished. Not only is she thinner, but her features have acquired a refined fineness . . .') When the couple, now the Duke and Duchess of Windsor, were married in France, in June 1937, Cecil Beaton was their official photographer; and just before the wedding he was given an exclusive sitting with the bride, for *Vogue*, at which she posed in her Mainbocher trousseau, and Schiaparelli's famous Surrealist

*Above* The Countess Haugwitz-Reventlow, née Barbara Hutton, the Woolworth heiress
HORST 1937

*Below* The Duchess of Windsor, photographed for *Vogue* soon after her marriage
HORST 1937

evening dress with a Dalí-inspired lobster design. Though the Windsors no longer had a clearly defined status in Britain, in France and America they were seen as uniquely glamorous leaders of society, and subjects of constant public interest. With its special entrée into the Duchess's world, *Vogue* was able to feed such interest, with formal portraits by Horst and Beaton, informal shots, and photographs of the Windsors' houses, beginning, in September 1938, with a rare feature on their life together at La Cröe, in the South of France.

In the wake of the Abdication, international society people were relieved to find that fashionable London life carried on unchanged. From the ending of the First World War onwards, the need for stability in a rapidly-changing world was a theme to which *Vogue*'s social columnists returned again and again. 'In a world as constantly-changing as our own, it is comforting to find some things as yet unaltered – the fashion for wearing tiaras, for example,' pronounced one contributor, in 1934. During the Great War, there had been gloomy predictions that social life in the old, grand tradition would never reappear; that great houses would be shut up, or destroyed, and the elegant formalities of fashionable entertaining be replaced by a drab and joyless set of democratic modes and manners; but as the 1920s progressed, such fears had proved to be unfounded. Some commentators continued to regret the vanished opulence of the pre-war era, with its sixteen-course banquets and rigid codes of behaviour; and there were constant complaints about the post-war difficulties of finding good domestic servants. ('For such gracious and womanly positions as cook, nurse, laundress, seamstress and maid – not so much as a single applicant will come,' sighed Dorothy Parker satirically in *Vogue* in 1919.) But throughout the 1920s and 1930s, the familiar rituals of bringing out debutantes in society, going to the Opera at the beginning of the season in tiaras and tails, and parading at the great race-meetings of Ascot, Longchamp or Belmont in clothes of elaborate frivolity,

Racegoers at
Longchamp
1934

The harbour at
Cannes
BEATON 1932

continued, unscathed by world events. The General Strike in Britain, in 1926, went almost unnoticed in the pages of *Vogue*. When France's first Socialist government was elected, in 1936, and national crisis threatened, the artist Vertès reported that the chic were wearing Schiaparelli's patchwork evening dress, taking to bicycles instead of Rolls-Royces, and trying to learn slang – but concluded wryly, 'All is as before.' Even the great financial crash of 1929, when fortunes were lost and depression followed, did not radically change society's outlook. 'It has suddenly become chic to be poor', American *Vogue* wrote cheerfully; 'you actually must suppress your riches in order to be in style.' Two years later, in the autumn of 1931, British *Vogue* asserted, 'Some of us are enjoying the New Poverty, and have developed an unsophisticated manner.'

As a concession to the times, American readers were urged to replace lavish entertaining with Sunday night hash suppers. British readers were recommended to forego foreign travel for the winter of 1931, in favour of more modest holidays at home – 'but some', the writer added, 'tell me they will winter in Egypt, because . . . Egypt has followed the Pound and is therefore to be encouraged.' The lure of travel was, it seemed, all but irresistible to the smart world. Everyone travelled, all the time: to Le Touquet and Deauville for the golf and racing, and St Moritz and Kitzbühel for the skiing; to Paris to choose clothes, dine out and see friends; to Cannes and Monte Carlo; Newport and Palm Beach; to Mexico, Morocco, Egypt. In *Vogue*'s society snapshots from all around the world, the same well-known faces constantly appeared – sunbathing on the Lido beach, picnicking at St Jean de Luz, doing gymnastics on the Riviera with the de Noailles' personal fitness instructor. Serge Lifar, star of the Russian Ballet, stayed at Syrie Maugham's 'Villa Eliza' in Le Touquet; Diana Vreeland, Elsa Maxwell and Elsie de Wolfe (Lady Mendl) were photographed with the d'Erlangers' house-party in Tunisia. Everywhere the 'society nomads' went, they were likely to meet their own set of friends; and though brief bathing-suits and cotton overalls might be the order of the day for the beach, the night-life in a resort such as Cannes required clothes, make-up and jewels fit for the Paris Ritz. Even en route, appearances had to be carefully maintained, and

*Vogue* showed clothes suitable for motoring, rail-travel, and flying. Travelling itself, whether by Blue Train, cruise-liner or zeppelin, had never been more glamorous; *Vogue*'s photographs and drawings conjured up a world of speed and luxury, in which helpful porters carried trunks and stowed cars aboard ships, and ocean voyages involved all the sophistication of the *Normandie*, or the *Queen Mary*.

Between New York, London and Paris there was a constant interchange of fashionable visitors. Since pre-war days, *Vogue* had kept its readers au fait with the social scene in smart foreign capitals, portraying a Paris of couture houses, chic women and fabulous entertaining, and a London steeped in grand tradition, with the potent allure of an aristocracy still presided over by royalty. There was keen interest in the fortunes of the many American heiresses who married into the British aristocracy, from Consuelo Vanderbilt, who became the Duchess of Marlborough in 1895, to the beautiful Thelma Morgan, who married Viscount Furness in 1926; and though not all the great Anglo-American alliances lasted, their descendants, such as the Astor publishing family, Lady Cynthia Mosley (first wife of the British fascist leader) and Winston Churchill ('the greatest Englishman since Disraeli') remained prominent in the social pages of the 1920s and 1930s. It was doubtless

The fashionable
traveller
MOURGUE 1929

with hopes of a titled mar[...]
mothers brought their daugh[...]
sented at Court and launched [...]
whether or not such a triumph [...]
curtseying before the King and [...]
of Buckingham Palace was gen[...]
experience for any young girl m[...]
the magazine's spring issues, [...]
were full of the London Season, with fashion for debutantes, guidance on palace etiquette, and reports of coming-out balls and Ascot appearances – so that readers everywhere were likely to be familiar with the details of the
length of train and shape of feathers to be worn at Court,
and how far ahead to apply to the Lord Chamberlain's
Office for the royal command to attend. For those who did
not live the life of international society, a copy of *Vogue*
provided a delightful window, through which to watch the
smart world go by.

*Above* 'Comfort in the sleeping-car'
PAGES 1929

*Below* 'A distinguished Anglo-American': Mr Winston Churchill with his wife Clementine, at Eaton Hall 1937

As unchanging as the Season's annual rituals was the all-
important sporting calendar. French *Vogue*, in 1926,
published a humorous 'Map of Chic', which showed how
'Le Monde Qui S'Amuse' pursued its sporting pleasures,
month by month, throughout the year, with skiing in St
Moritz in January, tennis and golf at Deauville and Le Touquet at Easter, fishing and shooting in Scotland in September, hunting at Pau in October, and so on. The centuries-
old traditions of blood-sports were kept up with undimi-
nished zeal by 1920s' and 1930s' society people. Nancy
Mitford wrote a witty article for *Vogue* in 1935, in which she
claimed that the Englishwoman's life between August and
April revolved entirely around 'The Great God Sport', as
she followed her husband between Scottish castles and
English estates, while he pursued his ruling passions of
grouse-shooting, pheasant-shooting, and fox-hunting. Such
passions were by no means exclusively masculine, however.
Beauties such as Lady Avice Spicer and Mrs Harold E. Talbott of New York were dedicated to hunting ('as she takes
her favourite dangerous fences I know she must be ex-
periencing a thrill of happiness', wrote Elsa Maxwell admir-
ingly of Mrs Talbott) and *Vogue*'s social features were full
of snapshots of determined-looking women in bowler hats
and well-cut breeches, at meets of fashionable hunts in

Mrs Nelson
Doubleday and
Mrs Harold E.
Talbott,
photographed on
Mrs Doubleday's
court at Oyster
Bay
HOYNINGEN-HEUNÉ
1929

England and America. Country-house parties were likely to include a shoot, at which women might join the guns, though for the more peacefully disposed, there were usually the rival attractions of croquet and golf, as well as tennis, to which leaders of society from the Duke of Westminster to Mrs Harrison Williams were devoted.

Dressing the part, whether for the hunting-field, the Côte d'Azur, or the Metropolitan Opera, was one of life's major preoccupations, in the world of *Vogue*. Hours would be spent with vendeuses and fitters; mannequins were scrutinised, fashion magazines scanned, every nuance of the season's collections studied. For women such as the Duchess of Windsor and the immaculate Mrs Reginald Fellowes, perhaps the most elegant of them all, to be perfectly dressed at all times was an overriding priority. Though *Vogue* published helpful features such as 'Smart Fashions for Limited Incomes', and 'Whispers to a Girl with Nothing a Year', fashion had everything to do with money and class, and little apparent connection with the world of the shopgirl or the stenographer, who were expected to copy the looks they saw in the magazines, or at the movies. Those who succeeded in entering the charmed circle from outside did so, almost invariably, by out-sophisticating society: the brilliant Josephine Baker, raised in ghetto poverty, was celebrated for her exquisite Vionnet dresses and fabulous taste in jewels; Noel Coward's droll, clipped hauteur endorsed, rather than challenged, the conventions of the privileged world which he both satirised and embraced.

Almost as great a preoccupation as fashionable dress, for the beau monde of the 1920s and 1930s, was fancy dress. At every opportunity, the chic would put on elaborate costumes, and become transformed for the night into characters from literature, figures from history, or their own opposite numbers. The costume ball was a tradition long beloved of society, with its roots in carnival and court masques – and both before and after the Great War, the theme of dressing-up recurred constantly in the pages of *Vogue*. 'The Bal du Grand Prix was the Splendid Climax of "La Grande Semaine" of Paris', American *Vogue* reported in 1922, describing the 'Bal de l'Opéra' at which guests such as Cécile Sorel and the Princess Joachim Murat had appeared in ravishing draperies of silver lamé and cloth of gold, adorned with masks, plumes, and all the trappings of bygone Venetian courtesans. 'Entertainments of this sort make it clear that Paris is maintaining its elegance,' noted *Vogue* approvingly. A year later, Paris continued to maintain its elegance with a lavish Opera Ball on a Chinese theme, and an 'unimaginably beautiful' ball given by the legendary Count Etienne de Beaumont, with costumes by Cheruit and Vionnet; while the highlight of 1927 was the Marchesa Casati's 'Fête Cagliostro', in her romantic rose-marble palace near St Germain, at which a sarcophagus carried in by four Egyptian servants turned out to contain the Duchess de Gramont. By the end of the 1920s, however, new young designers such as Cecil Beaton and Oliver Messel had picked up the torch, and opulence had begun to give way to modernity and wit. 'Do not be a Venetian lady if you can possibly help it,' Beaton ruled, adding firmly, 'All Eastern garments must be banned.' His suggestions for fancy-dress became increasingly daring and theatrical as the 1930s progressed, ranging from a black Surrealist costume covered with hands, to a headdress festooned with broken eggshells. The famously successful parties given by Elsa Maxwell took dressing-up to new heights: guests would be required to come as members of well-known families, or as one another, to everyone's mirth. ('I crave life and laughter as a duck craves water,' Miss Maxwell explained airily in *Vogue*.) Amid all the laughter, romance and glamour were never far away; and the decade ended with a wave of exquisitely staged fêtes – from Count Etienne de Beaumont's 'Racine Ball', and Lady Mendl's great 'Circus Balls' at Versailles, to the Georgian Ball at Osterley Park, in England, which was so successful that guests reassembled soon after to re-enact the occasion for the benefit of *Vogue*'s cameras.

By the end of the 1930s, the world was moving inexorably towards another world war, and the days of a leisured society, given up to its pleasures, were coming to an end. *Vogue* had largely ignored the Spanish Civil War, beyond publishing an anecdote about the royalist Duchess of Durcal's escape, dressed as a maid, which ended cheerfully, 'The Duchess, looking as chic as ever, told the story at a dinner in Paris.' The attempts of Sir Oswald Mosley and his brown-shirt supporters to establish fascism in England also passed almost without mention – although the spirited

*Above* The Hon Mrs Reginald Fellowes
HOYNINGEN-HEUNE 1932

*Below* The Indian Prince and Princess Karam Kapurthala, at the Racine Ball
HORST 1939

PARIS SPRING FASHIONS
WITH VOGUE PATTERN BOOK
MARCH 1940 (3) · PRICE 3/-

Vogue Carries On:
wartime *Vogue*
cover
PAGES 1940

Margot Asquith, Countess of Oxford, wrote bracingly in *Vogue* in 1936, 'We do not believe in mock-Mussolinis, silly shirts, self-advertising upstarts. We detest dictators.' In general, the attitude seemed to be that the Nazis should be ignored, as a bad joke. As late as the spring of 1939, after Hitler had marched into Prague, British *Vogue* continued to promise its readers a summer of 'pomp and pageantry in plenty for debutantes', with grand balls in great houses, and all the reassuring, unchanging, rituals of the annual social season. By July, however, the tone had changed. This season 'was memorable', the magazine wrote, 'for new values, and a new jumbled scale of living', and because 'all the world found time, inconspicuously, among its gaieties to do National service . . . fire-fighting drill, lorry-driving tests, Red Cross . . . and all the eligible young men at Territorial drill two or three evenings a week . . .' Reality, gradually, had begun to set in.

'*Vogue* – veteran of the last war, combatant in the present, proposes now to carry on,' announced the bold headline to British *Vogue*'s first editorial of the Second World War, in September 1939. Nothing, however, could have been more marked than the change in the magazine's tone since the Great War. Fifty years earlier, as young men were dying in the trenches, *Vogue* had written of *chiffons*, and how the officers on leave in New York were being practically smothered with comforts and 'canteening'. Now the mood was very different. Society women were no longer photographed in picturesque hats, with a few words on their 'strenuous' war-charity work appended to the caption; the columnists did not chatter of motor-shows and winter holidays. 'This New Year dawns on a world embattled and bleeding,' American *Vogue* wrote soberly in January 1941. 'What is *Vogue*'s place in such a world?' The answer was simple and practical: 'Our role now is essentially the same as it has always been . . . to report and reflect the activities of women – in peacetime or wartime.'

The activities of those who featured in *Vogue* had never been more varied, or more challenging. Jacqueline Cochran ferried aircraft to England; Mrs Reginald Fellowes, camping in the basement of Lady Diana Cooper's Mayfair house, became an air-raid warden, and added an axe and a gas-mask to her fabled wardrobe. Titled and fashionable British women were now shown in the severe uniforms of the WAAF or the WRNS, or in simple Utility clothes – checking lists of evacuees, working for civil defence, serving in mobile canteens. David Niven's wife, Primula Rollo, was a factory worker, making munitions; Lady Alexandra Metcalfe, married to the Duke of Windsor's friend 'Fruity' Metcalfe, was a St John Ambulance health inspector in the air-raid shelters. In the United States, society women flocked to support the war effort, joining the services, the Red Cross, Civilian Defense; and photographs in *Vogue* now showed society's leaders in their new roles – Mrs Vincent Astor, working for Navy Relief; Mrs Frederick Frelinghuysen, legendary hostess, applying her skills in a forces' canteen. Everywhere, women accustomed to a world of servants and luxury were discovering new talents and resources in themselves; new values and priorities.

Their lives, from day to day, would never be the same again.

Mrs David Niven,
née Primula Rollo,
munitions worker
1941

# WHY IS A DEBUTANTE?

'Who are these all-powerful beings?
What is a débutante? Why is she?'
VOGUE, July 1930

*Opposite*
Presentation
rehearsal: a
debutante
practises her court
curtsey under the
watchful eye of
Miss Vacani,
London's
celebrated dance-
teacher. Her dress,
'white tulle strewn
with gold stars', is
by Norman
Hartnell
RAWLINGS 1938

*Above*
Buckingham
Palace; *below*, the
Royal Procession
at Ascot
BEATON 1933

*Top* At Henley Regatta. 'During the Season, one frequently finds oneself beside the Thames – and one is sure to be there for the races'
FISH 1927

*Above* 'When their Majesties arrive at Ascot, in an old-fashioned landau, the band plays and there is a great bowing and scraping among the smart spectators'
FISH 1927

'The season, we know, belongs to the debutante,' wrote Nancy Mitford in *Vogue* in 1930; 'it is entirely for her sake that it happens, every year the same.' In the 1920s and '30s, the timeless, glamorous rituals by which eligible young women made their debut in society held an enduring fascination for *Vogue*'s readers – in America and France, as in Britain. Year by year, as each season approached, the magazine published photographs of current debutantes and reminiscences from their predecessors, advice on coming-out dresses, accounts of debutante dances, and notes on Court protocol for those about to be presented in London. 'We may all laugh at the solemn ritual we have inherited from the last century,' wrote Cecil Beaton, 'but we never allow it to be changed, though the housebreakers are heard in the land.'

The threats from such 'housebreakers' as strikes, socialism and economic depression were scarcely acknowledged in *Vogue*'s society pages. In the wake of the Wall Street Crash, one American contributor reported from London, 'Here one finds people still entertaining in the grand manner . . . *all* the silver is out, *every* room is in gala attire, and serried ranks of servants are in attendance.' As long as debutantes in feathered headdresses were still presented at Court, and footmen in powdered wigs and knee-breeches waited at grand balls, all seemed right with society's world. 'All this makes for glamour,' observed American *Vogue* approvingly, 'and helps to create a formula in the social life of an age that has no formulae otherwise.'

Much of the glamour of London's social formula resulted from the continued existence of a Court, and a season presided over by royalty. In Paris, coming-out was, by tradition, a discreet, almost sedate process: French debutantes, wrote *Vogue* in 1935, still led an 'antiquated, sheltered life', strictly shielded from publicity and often heading for an arranged marriage. The American debutante, in contrast, enjoyed a sophisticated, hectic existence, in which she was treated like 'a young film-star', besieged with invitations, and constantly spotlit in the press. Only in London did the 'serious social business' of coming-out have as its focus the gorgeous ceremony of curtseying to the monarch in the red-and-gold Throne Room of Buckingham Palace. The mystique of that occasion was heightened by the archaic style of dress which protocol demanded; whether the debutante's presentation gown was a skimpy knee-length model, as in the 1920s, or a 1930s column of flowing satin, it was accompanied by feathers worn in the hair, a veil and a regulation-length train. The business of managing a train and performing a sweeping curtsey was practised in front of mirrors and dancing-mistresses for weeks in advance – but still added to the debutante's terrors as she waited in the traditional pre-Court traffic jam, under the scrutiny of passers-by.

To the world at large, and debutantes in particular, the seasons offered a uniquely theatrical spectacle. Every year, the magazine's spring and winter issues described the same scenes and events with unfailing enthusiasm. Every year, debutantes, newly-emerged from finishing schools in Paris, Florence and Munich, were brought to town to meet their peers at dances, dinners and cocktail parties; to make their curtseys at Court; to attend the artistic highlights of the Metropolitan Opera and the Royal Academy, and go to the fashionable sporting fixtures – Longchamp and Ascot, horse shows and regattas. For three months, the capitals' streets were filled after dusk with 'a glittering galaxy' of party-goers – and caterers and restaurants flourished.

Increasingly, towards the end of the 1930s, *Vogue* contributors used the words 'industry' and even 'racket' in writing of the London Season. In 1939 an article entitled 'Data for Debs' openly conceded that it was possible, by payment to a suitable British sponsor, to 'arrange' to be presented at Court. ('This practice is very much frowned on,' the magazine wrote crisply.) But commerce had begun to vie with tradition as the hidden force behind the system.

In 1930, Nancy Mitford had whimsically answered her own question, 'Why Is a Debutante?' by referring to the business engendered by the Season; in 1939, as the last Paris and London seasons before the Second World War approached, an unusually sombre *Vogue* editorial declared, 'Whatever fears are felt or dangers threaten, we must go through with the gala; for what is sport to a few is daily bread to thousands.' The gala, however, was almost over.

*Above* 'The 4th of June, birthday of Eton College's founder, George III, is a great day, with fireworks, speeches and festivities. The boys all wear buttonhole bouquets'
FISH 1927

*Below* The curtsey
1927

# COMING-OUT IN NEW YORK

"The débutantes have claimed the winter season for their own. From the rise of the curtain on the autumn ball at Tuxedo (which, for many years, has sounded the official note for the chic débutante's first appearance), until the preliminary exodus for the South, these high-spirited daughters of the socially prominent have demanded that they be given the most elaborate form of entertainment that ingenuity could devise.

There have been 'teas' a-plenty, however, many in their own charming homes and others at the Colony Club. And there have been luncheons and dinners at Pierre's, Sherry's, the Plaza, and the Ambassador. But nearly all the imperious princesses, who have Midas-like fathers, have demanded a ball, and when they say a ball they mean it — showers of gold and everything the magical touch can command!

It is hard to recognize the tanned or freckled little girls one saw running up the beach at Newport or Southampton, not so long ago, in these very poised, chic young ladies receiving with their mothers at the head of the long stairway at the Ritz or other ballroom entrances. Simplicity is still the key-note of their costumes, but it is the simplicity of Lanvin, Vionnet, or Drecoll, which depends on its perfection of line and exquisite workmanship for effect and is far more costly than many elaborate models. From the top of her sophisticatedly cut hair to the tip of her Perugia or Hellstern slippers, every detail of the smart débutante's costume is perfection. Even the rose-leaf skin has not been guiltless of beauty creams or a touch of crimson lipstick (when mother wasn't looking), and, of course, the little powder-puff from the gold vanity-box is in frequent use, plus a whiff of expensive perfume.

A pretty custom that has been revived for débutantes is the use of the round bouquet. For several years, girls only wore shoulder bunches of orchids or gardenias, but now bushels of bouquets are sent to the débutante. Usually, she has them fastened to a tall screen behind her, as a background when she is 'receiving', but she also carries the one from the favourite young man or from her family, as the case may be, while she is dancing.

Among the characteristic notes of the times is the shortness of the débutante's dress. But, in spite of the strenuous exercise which has made this race of healthy young Amazons what they are to-day, they still have (with few exceptions) slender and shapely ankles, and one can't wish for the long dresses, pulled-in waists, and hothouse complexions of their grandmother's period.

During the month of December and the early part of January, there was a dance every night, sometimes four or five, and, in one evening, a swarm of boys and girls would rush from Pierre's to the Ritz, then to Sherry's or the Park.

To my mind, the only unpleasant feature of all these delightful entertainments is the unwieldy crowd of 'stags', who swarm in a mass right in the centre of the ballroom, like so many black-waisted wasps. Every little while, one of them detaches himself from the group and darts forward to snatch some girl from her partner's arms, but a good part of the time they just stand blocking the dancers and not adding much to the pleasure of others. How the girls stand it, is hard to imagine. With this cut-in system, the boys rest when they choose, but the popular girls never."

VOGUE, February 1927

*Left* Miss Grace Roosevelt, the daughter of Governor and Mrs Theodore Roosevelt. 'She made her debut at a brilliant party on Long Island'
VON HORN 1930

## COMING-OUT IN PARIS

*Above* 'Chaperon line-up: three French mothers appraise the debutantes' SCHALL 1935

*Opposite* Three French debutantes: Andrée de Montesquiou-Fezensac, Jeanne-Marie La Caze and Camille de Créqui-Montfort ANDRE DURST 1936

"Their pictures are never plastered over the society pages. Their fathers practically have apoplexy when their daughters' names appear in print. Their families don't squander a fortune in launching them. Better to put the francs in the dowry. They come out, these French débutantes, quietly at a little *'bal'* or still littler dinner, under the patriarchal roof.

They get in the Negro jazz orchestra from Florence's (they admit that no French orchestra knows a thing about jazz); order nice flowers and nicer food; and then proceed to check over the guest list with a sharp pencil.

Their first year out is definitely not a giddy, pampered, petted whirl. No unmarried girl – whether she's out one year or five – ever sees the inside of a night-club.

A good marriage is still her high purpose in life. After all, of what woman is that not true? About sixty per cent still accept docilely an 'arranged' marriage, but – times are improving – about forty per cent marry, if not for love, by mutual choice. They face the facts straight – careers are only fill-ins. If they have any furtive dreams of going on the stage or into the movies they might as well commit hara-kiri as mention them aloud.

What do they do with themselves? They go in heavily for sports now. And they're not dubs or dabblers at it, either.

For the first time in history they now have a club, the first club for unmarried girls to exist in France. It's called 'La Jeune Fille de France,' and is a branch of the Feminine Club of Arts and Letters, headed by the Countess Jean de Pange, formerly Princess de Broglie. The young twenty-year-old Princess Beatrice de Broglie is its first president. Thus under the holy name of arts, letters and charity French debs are now allowed wider activities.

They all dance well – waltz, tango, jazz, even a conservative Carioca. They smoke, spread on make-up with a cool, sure hand, are frank, poised, casual, modern – even though they still do little-girl curtsies to their elders, submit docilely to heavy chaperonage everywhere, pay dutiful visits to aunts and uncles, wear mourning, and never taste hard liquor.

They know that a crack has been made in their antiquated, sheltered life. Not a very wide crack, but they have hope – perhaps in the not too distant future life will begin at eighteen."

VOGUE, May 1935

# WHY IS A DEBUTANTE?
## by Nancy Mitford

*Above* Two Bright
Young Things,
seated on an
Italian sofa. Miss
Tanis Guinness *left*
wears a pale
mushroom-
coloured ballet
skirt a shade
darker than Miss
Baby Jungman's
'becoming chiffon
wisp'
BEATON 1928

*Opposite* One of
the most talked-
about debutantes
of her season:
Miss Elizabeth
Maugham,
daughter of the
novelist Somerset
Maugham and his
wife Syrie
Maugham, the
influential interior
designer. Miss
Maugham is seen
here 'in the
exquisite gown
which she will
wear for her
presentation'
PETER ROSE PULHAM
1934

" ' 'This year there are more important débutantes than ever before,' say the daily papers at the beginning of each London season in turn, and in this they are always right, because, of course, to themselves the débutantes are *much* more important than ever before, and to everybody else they are more than important — they are vital. Could the London season run its yearly course without the débutantes? They are the breath of its life, its chief if not its only justification, and each year they appear more important than ever before to prevent it from dying a natural death.

Who are these all-powerful beings? What is a débutante? Why is she?

A débutante is, of course, a young woman making her first appearance in society. But there is more to it than that, the word has other implications, and for some reason seems to carry us back to the agreeable atmosphere of the Edwardian days, when a girl was kept in the schoolroom until, round about her eighteenth birthday, a ball was given for her somewhere in the vicinity of Belgrave Square. Before this eagerly awaited occasion she met nobody outside her own family; after it she could meet those people selected by her papa and mama and in their presence. Tête-à-tête conversations with young men were discouraged until they took the form of a proposal, in the conservatory.

From those days the notion has come to us, so strongly imbedded in our minds that it is almost impossible to remove, that a débutante is a young girl, an immensely shy girl, chaperoned with untiring vigilance, who is savouring the delights of society for the first time. We look around us and wonder rather sadly where she is to be found.

Nevertheless débutantes in the proper sense of the word do exist even in 1930, although admittedly they soon escape from the restricting bonds of débutantehood. Dances are still given in Belgravia, the very chaperone is not entirely obsolete: she can yet be seen adorning the supper room with her seed pearl dog-collar and hen-with-duckling expression . . .

The present-day débutante would seem to have every advantage over her Edwardian prototype. In these days the débutante does as she pleases, with the result that everything she does she enjoys to the full.' "

VOGUE, April 1930

# DEBUTANTES, ENGLISH AND AMERICAN
## by Cecil Beaton

*Opposite* 'Miss Angela Dudley Ward in a fresh white frock, a camellia in her burnished hair, presents a picture of charm and sophistication exceptional even among modern debutantes'
BEATON 1934

*Below* One of the 'charming American debutantes who favour picture frocks': Miss Alice Moates, in her 'white tulle crinoline which the Callot sisters have ornamented with full-blown roses'
BEATON 1928

*Below right* An American debutante: Miss Natica Nast, daughter of Mr Condé Nast, the proprietor of *Vogue*, as she was presented at Court 1932

"Until she is sixteen, the English girl is rarely seen. Beribboned with pink bows, she may be produced as a sort of cabaret turn at the end of tea, but certainly she is never heard. Ordinarily, she wears black woollen stockings and a white blouse under a navy-blue serge uniform, low heels and a tight pigtail . . .

Rhoda is given her coming-out dance. There are lengths of red carpet laid to the kerb in Belgrave Square, red-and-white striped awning, a lot of bullet-hard cold chicken and a good deal of champagne . . . So Rhoda is launched, and her first season goes by. Now she is travelling to Cowes for the yachting, and we switch to the American debutante — who wears a sophisticated dress from Augustabernard and is as different from her European counterpart as root beer from beer.

In America, even though the girl and her mother consider the whole routine is the bunk, it is necessary to conform to the definite formalities to enjoy the title 'debutante' . . . At fourteen, there is the Senior Holiday Dance, and this gives way to the Metropolitan Dance, known as the 'Met'. If Susie does make it to the 'Met', she is practically out of the woods . . .

To be a fully qualified American debutante means a gruelling existence. Besides the glut of parties, committee meetings, incessant sittings for her picture, she is a member of the Junior League, which necessitates her being interested in welfare work. She must have a 'swell' time at the Yale prom. It is her business to be a social success, and she must be perpetually chased by the stags."

VOGUE, April 1932

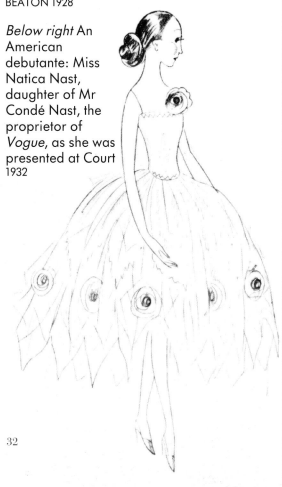

SCENE IN THE STUDIO
*Left* A behind-the-scenes picture of the photograph opposite, showing Cecil Beaton at work. The debutantes are accompanied by mothers, governesses, friends and family dogs: *left to right,* Viscountess Curzon, Piggie, 'Beckie', 'Mr Guppy', Marchioness Douro, Miss Stevens. Mr Cecil Beaton, assisted by Ninnie (up the ladder), photographs 'a glorious glut of loveliness'

*Opposite, left to right,* The Hon Georgiana Curzon, Lady Anne Wellesley, Miss Nancy Beaton and Miss Deidre Hart-Davis
BEATON 1928

# PRESENTATION NOTES
## by Lady Eleanor Smith

"Once upon a time, when women were presented at Court, they wore long veils that nearly reached the ground, vast trains that dragged behind them like peacocks' tails, and, whatever colour their frocks, compulsory white shoes and stockings.

Nowadays Court regulations are far less stringent, but it is unwise to choose an exceedingly short dress. Also, if you wish to be comfortable, insist upon a light train, as the greater part of your evening is spent in manipulating it. Some women carry a bouquet, or a feather fan; both of which look attractive and help a nervous débutante by keeping her hands occupied, but add rather to the responsibilities of the evening. As for the feathers, they must be white or black, and the tulle veil, which I cannot describe as attractive, must be white also. Personally I think that all this paraphernalia looks more attractive with a shingled head than not, as the feathers are attached to a narrow diamanté circlet, which clips neatly round the head. The train has to be two yards in length, and must stretch for eighteen inches along the floor.

Once inside the Palace the débutante remains wedged in a solid queue of people until her name is called out. She then moves, still in a long line, across the Throne Room. For one brief moment she sees the King and Queen in all their splendour, makes two low curtseys and files out. Her train will not bother her at all, for it is deftly unfurled by one gorgeous individual as she enters the Throne Room, and as deftly returned to her by another as she exits.

Everything is over, and the ordeal is not a very terrifying one, although at first the spectacle of so many hundreds of people in such dazzling dresses and such glittering uniforms is a little bewildering. There is, however, no need whatsoever for nervousness, and the scene is probably the most brilliant one in the world to-day."

VOGUE, April 1927

*Main picture* Presentation Day. *Left* Waiting in the ante-chamber for the summons to the Throne Room. *Below* 'The débutante advances to make her curtsy', in a gown of pale oyster satin
FRANCIS MARSHALL 1935

# LONDON TO NEW YORK —
# A DEBUTANTE-DIALOGUE

"*Eva:* I am so thrilled at the prospect of being in London for the season! Tell me all the things I am going to do.

*Vera:* The first thing you have to do is to go to Court and be presented.

*Eva:* But who will present me?

*Vera:* I have just been inquiring about that from the Lord Chamberlain's Office. Every American girl must be presented through her Embassy here. You will be presented by the American Ambassadress, who introduces a group of American women at each of the four drawing-rooms held during the season. In order to be presented by your Embassy, you must have letters from important political people in your own country — from your Senators, Cabinet Officers, or members of the Government — and they should be forwarded to your Embassy here to allow them to make the necessary arrangements.

*Eva:* I think Mother can arrange all that. But what sort of dress must I have?

*Vera:* You may wear any becoming evening dress. I saw a lovely Patou model in a recent issue of Vogue, all in white tulle . . .

*Eva:* What about my court train?

*Vera:* Oh, trains are much shorter now that short dresses are being worn. Your train should lie on the floor, eighteen inches from your heel. And, mind you, don't have your skirt too short; it is not liked at Court.

*Eva:* What about my hair and the feathers?

*Vera:* Oh, you just wear three small feathers at the back of your head and a short tulle veil held on by a little *diamanté* fillet or bandeau.

*Eva:* It all sounds very thrilling, but I know I shall be frightened.

*Vera:* Of course, you won't be frightened. American girls are never frightened. You all seem to have so much poise, and, besides, everything is made quite easy for you. When you are being presented, you come in through the huge gold doors, just behind the lady who is to present you. You mustn't get frightened and follow her too closely, else you might tread on her train. Your sponsor will make her curtsy just before you. And, as she is a friend of Their Majesties, they will probably shake her by the hand. Then, she will bow over their hands a second time, retreat a few steps, curtsy, and retire through the opposite door. You will follow her after you have made two curtsies — one to the King and one to the Queen. At Court, one makes a deep curtsy — not like the bob one makes on occasions when meeting the Prince of Wales or other royalties informally.

*Eva:* It sounds very dazzling. It must be a beautiful sight.

*Vera:* You will probably be dazzled by the glamour of it all, as it is your first experience. But your eyes will be on the King and Queen, so you will probably not notice that there are a great number of other people in the room . . ."

VOGUE, May 1927

# THEY WERE MARRIED
## by Cecil Beaton

*Below* Princess Nathalie Paley in a dress by Lelong, her husband FRANCIS MARSHALL 1928

*Opposite* Town Wedding: Mrs Peter Quennell, in gown by Enos HORST 1936

"The engagement is announced. The telephone bell peals incessantly. The front door bell rings. The postman brings a pile of letters by each post. There are enquiries and requests from caterers, photographers, jewellers, dressmakers, lingerie shops, hat shops, house agents and insurance agents. People that you had entirely forgotten about appear upon the scene, the household becomes completely disorganized. The bride is in a whirlwind. The wedding is to be in six months' time, the honeymoon is to be spent in New York and Honolulu — therefore, every sort of garment is necessary. The bride's father happily produces a cheque for the trousseau, for the quarterly dress allowance is now long spent . . .

It is fixed that the bride shall wear a Lily Elsie gown, and that the bridesmaids shall be slightly Edwardian, slightly Empire, slightly mediaeval, and shall be linked together with long garlands of flowers. The whole thing shall be chalk-white . . . The final sketches are made; everyone jumps with delight. The bridesmaids' eyes pop. The doorbell rings. Manley, the butler, brings in more presents. The bride, on her knees in the drawing-room, scribbles in her book . . .

The crowd is vast outside the church. I must say, the flowers are unbelievable. Never has St Margaret's, Westminster, looked so gay. More people arrive. 'Name please! Name please!' from the busy crowd of journalists chattering at the door. The organist pipes reedily. The pages sit in a back pew, wrapped in Shetland shawls with proud Nannies attendant. The bridesmaids flutter like doves. The bride's late . . . The church bells are clanging disturbingly, but at long last, from the reaction of the crowds outside, one can tell that the bride has been spotted. Necks crane — heads twist sideways.

The bridesmaids are roped with their flowers, the bride's veil and train patted, and the ceremony begins. The congregation knows of the rest. In the vestry we sign our names and excitedly kiss and congratulate each other, and then the procession walks down the aisle to the bellowing of the Wedding March.

Happily, there was no hitch — though newspapers reported that two policemen, three photographers, and several old ladies were knocked over in the scrum-scenes outside. But though the reporters dwelt upon the more sensational aspects, I have never witnessed a more reverent ceremonial, and I know I shall never forget the poignant beauty as the bridal cortège solemnly, and as if in slow motion, trooped out into the cold winter afternoon, and passed through into the court with the roofless trees against the blue stone of St Margaret's Church, the bride and her maids like Mélisandes in their long white draperies and dragging garlands."

VOGUE, May 1933

# THE BRIGHT FROTH OF ENTERTAINMENT

'Outsiders sometimes wonder what is the "Open Sesame" to the many-ringed circus where Insiders are disporting themselves so gaily. It is just the ability to ride about as they do, without getting dizzy.'

VOGUE, October 1923

*Left* First Night of a new film
ERIC 1930

*Right* The snake-dancers at Belle Livingston's Country Club
PAGES 1931

*Above* The
Spanish dancers,
Ramon and Rosita,
at New York's
Club El Patio – 'a
charming place to
spend the midnight
hours'
PAGES 1931

'To feed and to dance, always to be moving, that is the thing. We must move on. We must miss nothing', wrote Cecil Beaton in 1928, in one of his earliest articles for *Vogue*. As ever, Beaton captured the mood of the times. For many of those who appeared in his articles and photographs, social life was a ceaseless search for sensation, diversion, distraction, in which the fear of 'missing something' was matched only by the intolerable threat of boredom. To feed and to dance, to be permanently entertained, was the goal; and the 'monde qui s'amuse' seemed to be in a state of perpetual motion, whirling between cocktail parties and nightclubs, theatrical first nights and still more theatrical private parties. 'We daren't risk more than an hour or two in sleep', Beaton confided to his readers, 'in case something happens when we aren't there . . . '

Many of society's favoured meeting-places changed little from decade to decade. Covent Garden and the Met, theatres and concert-houses remained crammed with the fashionable, in evening-dress and diamonds; art exhibitions drew ever greater crowds, looking at one another as well as the exhibits, (as *Vogue* pointed out). At the Ritz in Paris, American, French and British habitués were greeted by the same punctilious maître d'hôtel, Olivier, who had waited on King Edward VII and Marcel Proust at the turn of the century. And in New York and London, while smart new restaurants dipped in and out of fashion, such landmarks of pre-war elegance as the Waldorf and the Savoy, or Prunier's, remained ever popular.

In the world of nightclubs, however, there was a constant demand for novelty: for new surroundings, new music, new frissons – from the exotic snake-dancer at Belle Livingston's Country Club to the scantily-clad circus cabaret at the Bal Tabarin in Montmartre. The 'extraordinarily chic' Embassy Club in London (the Prince of Wales's favourite) had, like its namesake in New York, an almost aloof grandeur; but at New York's vibrant Cotton Club, or the Boeuf Sur Le Toit in Paris, Park Avenue and Mayfair society rubbed shoulders with Bohemia. In an age of barely-concealed snobbery and racism, the skill and vitality of the black performers at the Cotton Club, or the Club Alabam', came as a thrilling revelation – and the smart world flocked to dine and dance in Harlem. 'Nègrerie' became a new craze; and from New York some of the best-known black entertainers went on to conquer Paris, where 'Bricktop' opened her own club, and Josephine Baker emerged as a major international star.

In private entertaining, as in public amusements, fads and fashions came and went. 'There have been "sailor parties", pyjama, end-of-the-world, Judgement Day, 1880s, dress-as-some-living-person Bottle Parties, and great fun they have been!' recorded Beaton in 1928. Scavenger hunts were a recurring craze. One, organised by Elsa Maxwell in Paris in 1930, was reported at length in *Vogue*. Among the objects to be rounded up by the laughing guests were a live duchess, a swan from the Bois de Boulogne and a pompon from a sailor's hat. The discomfiture of 'the startled sailor on guard at the Ministry of Marine', and his attempts to replace it (in 'terror of punishment' for being incorrectly dressed), were all part of the fun for the 'society scavengers'.

Any event organised by Elsa Maxwell was guaranteed to be a brilliant success. A stout, mannish American, her forte was fancy dress parties, at which she usually appeared in male attire – as Hindenberg, or President Hoover. Fancy dress was a ruling passion with the 'monde qui s'amuse', and balls and parties with every conceivable theme were described in *Vogue* – from the Count de Beaumont's romantic 'Racine' Ball in Paris, to Miss Maxwell's 'Come As Your Opposite' party in New York. The 'Circus Fête' which Lady Mendl held at Versailles in 1938 was so overwhelmingly successful that she gave a second Circus Ball a year later. That was in the summer of 1939; and for the smart world, the party was almost over.

Some of the best parties of the 1920s and 1930s were given by *Vogue*'s proprietor, Condé Nast, in his Park Avenue penthouse (decorated by Lady Mendl). In 1929, *Vogue* provided his recipe for successful entertaining. 'Mr Condé Nast's parties are pot-pourris mixed of one part Park Avenue, one part London and Paris, one part stage, opera and screen, one part the literary and artistic group. The success of this mixture is electrifying: there is a pleasant lift, a sustained excitement for even the jaded, and never, ever any let-down'. The writer might have been describing *Vogue* itself.

*Above* 'Mrs Harry Payne Whitney in black velvet with a bright green band in her hair looked particularly handsome as she listened to Mme Galli-Curci, newly engaged at the Metropolitan' 1922

*Right* At one of the season's most memorable parties, Lady Mendl's Circus Ball: seen in a corner of the ballroom, *front right*, Mr Tony Lawson lights a cigarette for M. Christian Bérard, the artist. Among the guests behind them are Mme Antenor Patino, in patterned gown, and Mlle Cécile de Rothschild
SCHALL 1938

*Opposite* Seven bachelor hosts, including M. Charles de Beistegui, gave a brilliantly glamorous party at the Sporting Club in Paris; their guests included Lady Abdy, whose 'glimmering white costume was completed by a diadem and ruche of white osprey'
HOYNINGEN-HEUNE 1932

# NOTES ON PARTYGIVING
## by Elsa Maxwell

"The making of a successful party is like the baking of a wonderful soufflé – the ingredients and proportions must be weighed and measured by the hand of an artist – should be taken out of the oven at exactly the psychological moment – and *served hot*. Carefully studied effects must appear just to happen, and the joy of the hostess in her own party must be the first element encountered by a guest.

Guests should be selected with as much care as a new Reboux hat, and should be equally becoming, for a hostess should wear her guests at a party as she wears a hat – with an air!

Ruthlessness is the first attribute towards the achievement of a perfect party. Also, one should have practically no really established 'position' – by that, I mean in the world of finance – religion – or diplomacy.

If you are officially associated with any of these worthy métiers – then give up the idea for ever of achieving a party, for official functions should be added to the list of Horrors of the Inquisition.

Never show the slightest anxiety about the ultimate success of your own party. Show, by your attitude, that you are convinced it will be the best party ever given, and your guests will believe it too, and help to make it so. A new idea, plus a sense of humour, makes a party – and bores break it."

VOGUE, July 1930

*Opposite* Ring Night at London's Covent Garden. 'Furtwängler conducting. Air vibrating with crash of Wagnerian chords. Boxes aflutter with people whispering, spotting friends, and (occasionally) listening to the music'
BEATON 1937

*Left* A Musical Evening in New York — listening as Mrs Bradford Norman Jr plays are Mrs William Averell Harriman, Mr Edward McIlvain Jr, and Mr John Kennedy. The sensational black-and-silver screen in the background is by Drian
STEICHEN 1933

# MUSICAL NOTES
## by Alan Pryce-Jones

"There is no reason to suppose that the prodigies which our grandmothers performed on the harp, or the madrigals which our remoter ancestors sang in their half-timbered manor-houses, were other than most unpleasant performances. But until quite lately, this kind of musical party was extremely fashionable. 'A little music' was a very normal way of spending the evening. It largely depended on the flirtatious gambit of lending somebody songs, and it was upheld by a secondary gambit of leaning on a piano while the charmer sang.

At last, the professional musician came into his own. People realized that — just as one does not call in an amateur surgeon or an amateur tailor — there is no special reason to rely on amateur musicians. If some people enjoy making their own suits or their own music, it is a pleasure, the world had decided, which must be kept private. So now the standard has risen high enough to make the giving of a musical party a hazardous enterprise.

During the Season one has only to open a newspaper to see with what a galaxy the musical hostess has to compete. Perhaps Lady Cory has had Kreisler to play for her; or the Austrian Minister has had a rival party on the opposite side of Belgrave Square. The sedate music of the Quartet Society floats out of Wimborne House and mixes with a saucier tune from the Ritz next door. The Duke of Marlborough has lent his house to a Concert Club. And, under each name, the paper goes on to give solid evidence of the beauty and distinction which graced each party."

VOGUE, October 1933

*Opposite* Side-show at the Bal Tabarin
ERIC 1937

*Right* Josephine Baker – 'soon to appear in the Ziegfeld Follies' – in gold-paper fantasy dress by Antoine
LOUISE DAHL-WOLFE 1935

*Left* Night life
WILLAUMEZ 1936

*Below* A legendary
entertainer, a
famous Paris
nightclub: Kiki
sings at the Boeuf
Sur le Toit in
Montmartre
ERIC 1927

# IN THE NIGHTCLUBS OF PARIS

"Josephine Baker has just arrived from the Folies Bergères, where she is playing, accompanied by her maid, her chauffeur, a white Eskimo dog and several nondescript people. She has come in without a wrap, and the length of her graceful body, which is 'light sealskin brown,' is swathed in a full blue tulle frock with a bodice of blue snakeskin and she has slippers to match. The frock is cut excessively low in the back, and there is a huge diamond ornament at the waist. She wears, on her left hand, an enormous diamond ring and on the wrist of the same hand a very impressive diamond bracelet. Her hair, which naturally grows in tight curls, is plastered close to her head with white of egg and looks as though it were painted on her head with black shellac.

As she appears in the new review at the Folies Bergères, one is struck by her great decadence of line. When, in the finale, she wears only a diamanté maillot of tulle and red gloves with diamond balls hanging from the tips of her fingers, she is the most extravagant thing in the most extravagant review that Paris has yet produced.

After she has danced, we go to her dressing-room . . . She talks of her success in Paris and what it means to her family back in Harlem, the negro quarter of New York. We admire her dress. She begs us one day to come to see some of her new costumes, one of which is made of snakeskin and such-like materials which match her complexion. She tells us that her new Voisin town car is painted brown — her brown — and that it is also upholstered in brown snakeskin. The dressing-room walls are covered with her photographs."

VOGUE, May 1927

*Right* Shades of
Toulouse-Lautrec:
the Bal Tabarin, in
Montmartre. Even
in Paris, where
brilliant, and
Bohemian,
nightclubs
abounded, the Bal
Tabarin was
famous for its
spectacular
floorshows.
ERIC 1938

*Opposite* 2.30 a.m.
in New York –
'They're snapped
against El
Morocco's byword
zebra upholstery.
Mrs Sherman
Jenney poses in a
dolman cape, with
a huge silver fox
muff. Mrs William
Wetmore sits for
her picture in a
very feminine
dress of tulle'
HORST 1938

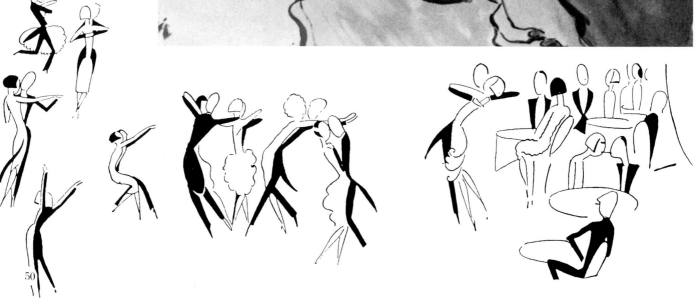

# 'DESIGN FOR LIVING' – A NEW PLAY FROM NOEL COWARD
## by David Carb

"Leo, one corner of the triangle which is the frame and the substance of Noel Coward's new comedy, *Design for Living*, is a playwright. The first scene of the second act takes place the morning after the London – and world – première of Leo's latest play. He reads the reviews to Gilda, who happens to be living with him. One of the reviewers describes it as 'thin. The characterization falters, but the dialogue is polished, nay brilliant.' That well describes *Design for Living* itself, and one need not be a psychologist to surmise that Coward meant it to. He would delight in 'beating the critics.'

Coward plays Leo. His performance is rich, scintillant. By the happy combination of a provocative personality, a finished technique, and an ingredient resembling magic, he creates a character which stirs the imagination – a rare example of high and ironic comedy that etches itself on the memory.

Alfred Lunt and Lynn Fontanne are co-starred with Coward. The performance of the former seems less good than it is because of being in constant contrast with superior playing. Beside the young British dramatist's suave, polished, yet emphatic acting, Lunt's florid style suggests a circus poster beside a Corot.

Miss Fontanne's acting, while far above all but the best on our stage, is inferior to her work in recent years. True, Gilda is overwritten and not clearly characterized, but in the rendition, she is more verbose and less sharply defined than the author wrote her. But those defects do not decrease her histrionic stature materially – she remains one of the two or three serious contenders for the title of leading lady of our theatre.

Leo's drama is dubbed a 'three-sided erotic hodge podge.' That phrase fits *Design for Living* also – erotic, mad, but enveloped by true humour."

VOGUE, March 1933

*Opposite* 'In this enthusiastic theatre party we see a conscientious performance of the role the perfect audience should play, which is a mixture of glamour and appreciation. The glamorous note is brilliantly struck by the ladies'
STEICHEN 1935

*Below* The 'hysterical closing-scene' of *Design for Living*, Noel Coward's new play
PAGES 1933

# SURREALISTS AT THE MUSEUM OF MODERN ART

"It has been the winter for the art dealers, and not only on Saturday afternoons are the galleries jammed. Derain is, of course, a prize draw, and Dali is now a name known to all. Between two and three thousand people went to see the Matisse at the Valentine Gallery. The Le Nains benefited charity and Knoedler's, and the multitudes who went to Seligmann's talked about pink-and-blue Picasso heaven. But after they had faded, since ten years in Paris, it has been the winter of the Surrealists. The afternoon tea-sets made of squirrel's fur, the young girl made of mouse-traps, have been carefully preserved, brought to the Museum of Modern Art, and have raised Cain. The baffled crowds mount the stairs, few differentiating between the excellent Chiricos and the wretched Tanguys, but, when they attain the highest rooms and see the work of the fourteenth and fifteenth centuries with the same symbols used, it is difficult for them not to feel the contemporary lack of invention and general disintegration of modern art.

At the opening of the show birds were caught in flight in women's hair. Black nail enamel made fingers look as though they had been caught in door-lintels. Mrs Sandy Calder looked out, as though wanting to escape, from the bird-cage of her husband's jewellery. Miss Leonor Fini, a negroid 'Bubbles,' ended up the evening by putting a chicken bone in a flower vase. Surrealism has swept the country like a plague. People are conscious, now, that pianos have cuticles and orchestras skins, that rooms must be soft and hairy, and that every one is suffering from paranoia."

VOGUE, February 1937

*Opposite* Varnishing Day. 'Princess Edmond de Polignac has recently revealed to us her talent as an artist. The recent exhibition of her works showed her to be a sensitive painter.' She is seen here with a fellow-exhibitor, Marcel Vertès – well known to *Vogue*'s readers as an illustrator SCHALL 1935

*Below* 'It is now the smart and amusing thing to go to galleries' PAGES 1929

*Left* The Surrealist Show at the Museum of Modern Art in New York BEATON 1937

# COCKTAILS AT SIX

"This is the open season for cocktail parties. You hear people say that they hate cocktail parties, that they never go. But cocktail parties go on unabated. There is hardly a day when anybody in London society does not have an invitation to cocktails – and they are becoming a very highly specialised form of entertainment. It is the hour of new hats and new food. Just before six o'clock all the smart women return home to change their hats, before starting out for their cocktail rendezvous. Yes, you must now have a hat consecrated to the cocktail hour.

Nowadays, the high point of any cocktail party is not so much the cocktails as the food that goes with them. Imagination about cocktail party food has become an absolute necessity – and to copy your clever friends the sincerest form of flattery. At this time of the year some hot food is essential – but nothing so unimaginative as hot sausages. They are out of date, back numbers. You must think up something different. The Prince of Wales has hot buttered American soda biscuits, with cod's roe, served in hot silver breakfast dishes, and creamed shrimps in little pastry containers. Mrs Maugham has hot bacon sandwiches, which disappear as fast as the cook can make them. Lady Portarlington has a cocktail size edition of a hot meat pie, which nobody else has yet thought of (have you ever noticed that it is always the same people who think of the new things first?). Of course, it would be Mrs Ernest Simpson who first thought of the wonderful combination of seeded white grapes with little cubes of Dutch cheese, stuck through with a wooden toothpick. Mrs Simpson's food is of such a high standard that the intelligent guest fasts before going to dine or to have cocktails with her. Her hot dishes at cocktail parties are famous and are passed around in small quantities at intervals."

VOGUE, December 1935

*Opposite* Cocktails at the 500 Club, 'a favourite rendezvous for the cocktail and sandwich meal that refreshes some of our most crowded days'. Seen here are Mrs Plunket Greene – 'wearing one of the new feathered hats' and, *centre* Mr Brian Howard HOWARD AND JOAN COSTER 1929

*Below* The quintessential cocktail party ERIC 1928

*Above right* At Elsa Maxwell's 'Come As Your Opposite' party in New York: Miss Maxwell, as President Hoover, and Mrs Harold E. Talbott 'as the Broadway siren, Diamond Lil'
VON HORN 1931

*Above* A Surrealist costume designed by Cecil Beaton
BEATON 1937

*Right* Cecil Beaton impersonates the ethereal Lady Mendl
1934

# SUGGESTIONS FOR FANCY DRESS
## by Cecil Beaton

Apollo
BEATON 1954

"What about putting your head into a bag of gold net? What about pinning roses from your great-aunt's hat all over your cherry-coloured velvet evening jacket, and cutting white kid leggings above the knees, to go as a garden boy? What about taking all your coloured handkerchiefs and bandaging your entire body? What about hanging a gold frame around your shoulders and calling yourself a portrait?

Fancy-dress fashions are ever-changing. To-day, at no cost must the costume cost much. It is embarrassing to appear in anything elaborate. To appear effective as the result of a last-minute brain-wave is the great achievement, for the slight and unpretentious gesture is necessary.

Mrs Mencken has monopolized the Queen of Sheba, and a former Mrs Hutton is unsurpassable as Marie Antoinette, so that now an effective grandeur can only be legitimately achieved with every-day utensils, and materials being used for purposes for which they were not meant. Steel wool pot-cleaners, egg-beaters, egg-separators, dish-cloths, tin moulds, and patent hangers all make excellent costume trimming. Even Queen Elizabeth is permissible if her farthingale is made of cane matting, her crinoline of the stuff that is hung up around the shower, and her jewellery of shells and cork covered with tinsel.

This is not perversity. An effect is created only by the unexpected and provocative. Anybody who can afford it can hie himself to a hire shop, and at great expense in proportion to the effect which it will create, acquire still another fancy-dress costume. By taking a tour throughout the variegated counters of any big store, with fancy dress written

on the mind and five dollars in the pocket, it is possible to find innumerable materials that can be misused with effect.

Mr Oliver Messel has an astonishing knack of reducing brown paper sacking to something pliant in his hands. Bérard was the first to cut eighteenth-century coats out of furnishing tapestry, so that lovers frolicked over the shoulder-blades and cupids blew a fanfare over the hips. As with many other costume ideas, the influence was felt in the world of fashion, and tapestry coats were introduced by Alix in the rue du Faubourg Saint-Honoré. Costumes that have originated from Jean Cocteau strike a sinister note, and are reflected in the sequin eyebrows and pouting mouths stamped on veils in Schiaparelli's Collection.

Masks never lose their magic. The conjurer's trick shop is a treasure-trove. Broken eggs are as pretty as daffodils and much more unusual. Imitation spilt ink makes a pretty motif. A beautiful late-Victorian coiffure can be made of sausage-curls that are real sausages, with posies of rubber fruit or even rubber lamb-chops.

And for the more solid forms of costume, the variegated designs of candlewick bedspreads in all colours open a new field. For clinging draperies, oiled silk (meant for bathrooms), figured and otherwise, is wonderful, once the smell has worn off. Vegetables (artichokes, in particular), the roots of plants, and packing paper have their other uses. Bring out forgotten flowers, forgotten materials. Stick to the lower classes and keep the bill down. Then only will your costume be remembered!"

VOGUE, December 1937

*Left* 'Miss Consuelo Villa, daughter of Count and Countess Alfonso Villa, throws her loveliness into sharp relief with a fantastic, completely original headdress, splashed with imitation broken eggs from a toy-shop'
BEATON 1937

*Right* At one of Elsa Maxwell's most amusing parties – Mrs Robert L. Stevens in costume as 'a very young Greta Garbo'
STEICHEN 1930

*Opposite* 'Sovrani's restaurant at lunch-time sees some of the most chic gatherings in London.' At the far table, on the left, is Lady Dunn, just come from a strenuous sitting for Augustus John, who is painting her and her husband. In the foreground, Mrs Robin d'Erlanger and Mrs Bendix are lunching with Mrs Thursby, after a charity committee meeting
HOWARD AND JOAN COSTER 1929

*Left* Olivier, maître d'hôtel of the Ritz in Paris, and a well-known gourmet, Mr Berry Wall
ERIC 1936

# MAÎTRE D'HOTEL

"To have a famous maître d'hôtel greet you respectfully by your surname, to greet him in turn familiarly as Olivier, Albert, Pierre, or Paul, is a strong tonic to your ego. For, in his own mise en scène, a maître d'hôtel is a person of importance; he is a diplomat, a big executive, a master waiter, a culinary and wine expert, and a psychologist.

Olivier is the doyen of maîtres d'hôtel; he is legendary – he is a personage of his age – an age that is quickly passing. He himself says with sadness that every year the list of his old clients diminishes; those who are left are marked by changed fortunes. The long list of royalty that he served hardly exists as such any more.

However, changing times and changing manners have not changed Olivier's discrimination. He can still discern at a glance the worth of a new guest. He can seat a conspicuously vulgar woman inconspicuously and do so in a manner that will convince her that she occupies the best position in the room. He can seat notables so that their privacy is assured, and yet every one else in the room is conscious of their presence. And, being essentially kind-hearted, despite the necessary snobbism of his profession, he can seat nobodies so that they feel they are personages.

He is at the door to greet every guest, he is never hurried, never fussed. He is the perfect maître d'hôtel."

VOGUE, January 1936

*Below* Lady
Warwick dining at
the Mayfair Hotel
in London
FRANCIS MARSHALL
1935

# DINING OUT IN LONDON

"If on any winter's evening you could peer through the walls into the private lives of almost any family in Mayfair, Belgravia or South Kensington, you would find the entire household busily preparing to entertain, or to go out and be entertained. So confirmed is now this habit of filling our evenings that we stay at home only to receive, and the tradition of 'three nights a week out' – which pre-supposed three gay evenings and the remaining four spent by the fireside with a book – has been quite superseded. When the Parisian goes out he makes a night of it, returning only with the dawn (hence the reputation Paris has for late nights). But then the Parisian goes out rarely, while though Londoners come home to bed moderately early they go out every night. And so it is the fulness of life at night, rather than its lateness, that helps to create the glamour of a London that is now the envy and astonishment of the rest of the world. Look at it how you will – and nobody has quite explained this rising tide of London gaiety – the fact remains that London has never before been so thrilling after dark.

If you listen to the conversation of the foreigners at the next table – naturally expecting much more critical comment than the Englishman would allow himself – you will be certain to hear them tell each other how wonderful the food is (as they savour the pheasant cooked in cream and some of the wonderful wines from the Savoy cellars). You will hear them discussing the pretty women coming into dinner and the comment probably is that although so good-looking and well-dressed, most English-women are very badly coiffed. In Paris, you must remember, they are used to women with hair dressed in an exquis-

itely neat way that really isn't at all the fashion in London.

When you have done with looking at your neighbours, you will be vastly entertained by the turns of the cabaret show that comes on about 9.30 – really excellent turns, the like of which can't be bettered in any music hall. What the famous American producer, the late Flo Ziegfeld of the 'Follies' did for the American girl, i.e., glorify her, every London restaurant keeper open at the supper hour now does for the girl in general, making her his chief attraction (very Edwardian, this)."

VOGUE, November 1934

# DINING OUT IN NEW YORK

"When Dusk falls like crumpled black tulle over the city and the belated evening breeze begins to stir, women in penthouses and men in sky-scraper offices, débutantes stranded in apartments overlooking the East River, and young gentlemen sated with bond selling, raise, like a jazz anthem, the question, 'Where shall we go to-night?'

Shall we be quite grand and wear the white crêpe and the round turquoises to sophisticated surroundings and dance to a tail-coated orchestra? Shall we be a little less swell and wear the beloved mauve chiffon to a cool, quiet place with dreamy waltz music and dim corner tables? Shall we dress hurriedly in thin black and a crystal necklace and go the rounds of two or three amusing little places with curious settings and diverting entertainment? Or shall we keep on the printed afternoon dress and the shiny straw beret and motor to a roadhouse through the delicate night-air of the country?

Perhaps, it is the white crêpe in which one emerges on the streets of a pleasure-

bent city. One dines at the Persian roof-garden of the Ritz, where the walls are painted to seem a delectable Persian paradise, into which one almost could walk. Theodor stands at the door, a benign and charming genius of the place. Between delicious brook-trout and alligator-pear salad, one dances to a very paragon of orchestras, inspiring, yet miraculously soft, with an alluring drummer who weaves a tangle of syncopated tempo. Back at one's table, one sips water from the dark blue glass goblets that are a trademark of all the Ritzes; one whispers an invitation to tea next day to an acquaintance at a neighbouring table; only too soon is it found to be half-past ten, and one calls regretfully for the check."

VOGUE, July 1930

*Above* The Duchess of Windsor, in sophisticated black lace evening gloves, dines out in Paris at the Ambassadeurs
EGGARTER 1938

*Previous page* After dinner, coffee on the terrace
PAGES 1931

*Opposite* The snack bar of the Blue Train Grill
ERIC 1934

# THE JOYS OF TRAVEL

'Today, we are accustomed to thinking of the smart world as a carefree band of extravagant gypsies, whose unceasing trek and bright temporary encampments are accompanied by every gaiety.'

VOGUE, June 1928

*Right* 'She takes off in a Jean Patou suit that won't crush en route.' Her alligator bag, by Hermès, contains a hidden jewel case
ERIC 1936

*Left* Tunisia, an oasis of the south
1929

'There was a time', a *Vogue* article of 1928 began, 'when the hallmark of the smart world was its static quality.' Then, 'only the cheap rich careered through the continents in search of pleasure . . .' By the early 1920s, however, society's attitude to travel (as to so much else) had changed; and as the decade progressed, the fashionable world became, in *Vogue*'s words, 'a nomad tribe', constantly journeying, 'like extravagant gypsies', from one colourful encampment to the next. By boat, train and plane, from Palm Beach and the Venice Lido to the French Riviera and Tunisia, the society gypsies were always on the move; and in the decades between the wars their ceaseless trek provided inspiration for *Vogue*'s photographers, writers and artists.

Wherever they went, they took their own way of life with them. Along the French Riviera, little fishing-villages were rapidly transformed into sophisticated resorts, with modern villas, tennis-courts, smart restaurants, and casinos. In America's long-established 'sunlit playground' of Palm Beach, traditional cottages were ousted, after the War, by Mediterranean fantasy-mansions, built (or inspired) by the society architect Addison Mizner, and presided over by Huttons and Vanderbilts, the Otto Kahns and the Harrison Williamses. 'Impossible to believe that the slump has occurred!' marvelled Cecil Beaton in 1931, reporting for *Vogue* from the idyllic sunlit scene, where swimming and the beach life by day gave way, at night, to an opulent world of nightclubs, chic restaurants and 'gambling saloons'.

From Palm Beach, Newport and Southampton to the cities and resorts of Europe, the nomad tribe trekked on. According to taste and season, they might migrate to Paris, to see friends and buy clothes; to Tunisia, to join Elsa Maxwell and Diana Vreeland in a house-party at the d'Erlangers' exotic villa; to Antibes, for sun and relaxation at the new Eden Roc Hotel. Then on to Venice, where Lady Diana Cooper might be seen gliding, half-hidden by a parasol, in a gondola, or Christian Bérard could be observed sketching Chanel as she sauntered, in fake *bijoux* and flowered beach-pyjamas, across the gilt sands of the Lido.

Fashions that started in the chic resorts were rapidly taken up by the rest of the smart world. At the Lido Beach, cotton

*Below* Travel – a
*Vogue*'s Eye View
SCHALL 1934

mechanics' overalls in jaunty colours became the stylish alternative to shorts or brief bathing-costumes. Along the Riviera, spotted kerchiefs, peasant straw hats and striped fishermen's sweaters, as worn by local workers, were snapped up by women whose holiday luggage included fortunes in jewels and Vuitton trunkloads of couture clothes. Exotic travels yielded still greater rewards: after Elsa Schiaparelli's 1936 trip to Tunisia (during which she was photographed in Berber costume for *Vogue)*, she returned to Paris to create an inspirational Arabic collection – which included prototype, deep-soled, platform shoes.

The craze for sunbathing which Coco Chanel had helped to popularise in the 1920s had begun to be questioned by the 1930s. *Vogue* issued caveats about the effects of sun on skin, and advocated careful use of creams and lotions. The fashion for health and fitness remained, however. Society's favoured resorts offered tennis, golf, and watersports as well as cocktail bars and nightclubs; *grandes dames* and elder statesmen, as well as Bright Young Things, acquired tans and sporty beach clothes; even such redoubtable figures as Lady Mendl were photographed on holiday performing acrobatic exercises, with the aid of a muscular fitness instructor. 'The physical instructor, a kind of "super-thug", is the new fashion, introduced by the Vicomte de Noailles,' *Vogue* reported from the Riviera in 1926, adding, 'We are certain to hear more of this new fad of acrobatic parties.'

The search for sensation and diversion was unceasing. Society's travellers visited the pyramids of Egypt, and Soviet Russia; booked on the maiden-voyages of great cruise-liners; even – like one of *Vogue*'s own contributors – flew in the *Hindenberg*, before its dramatic explosion called a halt to airship expeditions. Apart from actual dangers, travel had its drawbacks (as the cartoonists pointed out), in the form of passport queues, cramped accommodation, and comical, uncomprehending foreigners; yet, as Evelyn Waugh wrote in *Vogue,* 'one remembers, in an agreeably exaggerated form, the pains and dangers; the boring days fade out.' During the 1920s and '30s, wanderlust had become a way of life for fashionable society; and the 'organised restlessness of present-day existence', engendered by one war, was only to end with the outbreak of another.

*Above* Taking one's car to Europe: 'the day before the steamer sails, the car is swung up over the side and deposited below deck' 1927

# THE SOCIETY GYPSIES

"There was a time – *Vogue* remembers it – when the hallmark of the smart world was its static quality. You knew where and when to find it at home. Only the cheap rich careered through the continents in search of pleasure; the pursuit of health and the invitation of relatives were then the only excuses for the really good people leaving their town houses in winter and their country houses in summer.

Then something happened – the War. Families were broken up, ties were severed, and incomes were halved, quartered, and horribly mutilated. The whole world took to wheels, to a greater personal independence, and, as the years slipped by, to a fundamental need for change, for movement, and for getting out of a precarious life what it could, while it could. It was then that the great nomadic tribe of smart people came into being. Freed from the superstition that one cannot travel without a caravan of servants, that travel is an undignified enterprise, and that to be a respectable and cultivated member of society one must not know too much about anything, the smart world left home.

To-day, we are accustomed to thinking of the smart world as a care-free band of extravagant gypsies, whose unceasing trek and bright temporary encampments are accompanied by every gaiety. The organised restlessness of present-day existence approximates more and more to that of the veritable gypsy, who meets his brethren and puts up by the roadside at stated seasons of the year for State Fairs. The very cities of Europe themselves begin to resemble villages, so all-embracing is the informal hospitality of to-day, so easily overcome are all distances, and so indistinct all boundaries within the *monde qui s'amuse.*

So is it on any night in Paris, London or New York; so is it again on the sun beaches of the Riviera, in the bars of the Côte d'Argent. The same cars, the same people driving up like sheep in their flocks, yet not an eyebrow nor a voice is raised in surprise at finding one's friends so far away from what used to be called home. These are the State Fairs of the Society Gypsies, these are their annual encampments. By the end of the summer, their very swarthiness is reminiscent of their Romany prototypes, and always where they put up, loud music and lively dancing, vivid clothes, and a galaxy of shining ornaments make brilliant the surrounding night."

VOGUE, June 1928

*Opposite* When in Rome . . . The beautiful Princess Eugenio Ruspoli beside the Trevi Fountain
HOYNINGEN-HEUNE 1933

*Left* Mrs Littletown of America, seen before – and after – her first trip to Paris
1924

*Below* 'Where the smart world is to be seen – along the rue de la Paix, crossing the Place Vendôme'
MOURGUE 1927

# VISITING PARIS
## by Mary Bromfield

"The visitor to Paris is a sightseer, shopper, passer through, or, as a rule, all three together (besides being an eater and drinker), in one of the most beautiful cities of the world, where there are certain definite things that she feels have to be done. Her time, long or short, is taken up in seeing the sights she wants or feels she ought to see; going into every conceivable nook or cranny where the antique or modern can be looked at and bought; looking at, trying on, and fitting clothes, then taking them back to begin again, in the wild hope of making them better; eating and drinking in restaurants, cafés, and bars, large and pretentious or small and whispered about (the kind that for some inconceivable reason, you quite naively believe no one else has ever heard of); and, of course, seeing friends, French or American, and doing and seeing what they want to do and see. It is all exciting and amusing (if exhausting), even to an old-timer who does it once or twice every year. The climate and the breakfasts, unless you have come there to make a study of just such things, pass by almost unnoted . . ."

VOGUE, January 1930

# THE BADEN-BADEN CURE
## by Cecil Beaton

*Above* 'The solemn ceremony of drinking Baden water'
BEATON 1929

"Did you ever take a cure? No? Then let us suppose, for the moment, that you have chosen Baden-Baden, appreciated centuries ago by the Romans for its thermal waters; now elaborated by the Germans; and patronized from March till November by titled Europeans, and by fashionable Americans who do not have to count the cost. Here, to this really picturesque town lying amid the pine-wooded hills of the Black Forest, you may come to lose unwanted kilos, to gain in weight, or to quiet jumpy nerves. Or – merely to come to a luxurious *Badeort*, if you have fallen into that self-indulgent habit.

You may go to a good hotel – be attended by a kindly, competent German physician – and follow his régime with the assistance of the maître d'hôtel, the *Trinksaal,* and the state thermal baths. This is unquestionably the most comfortable method and brings good results if you have the persevering will to follow instructions without the reminder of formal institutional restrictions. In all probability, you will play the game squarely. For you came to Baden-Baden expressly for this *Kur*, and your faith is unshaken. You will be encouraged, also, by the good example of others, likewise going at stated times to take the prescribed walk or bath or massage. A cheerful band holds concerts (the first of four in the day), from seven-thirty until nine of a morning, while men and women of diverse shapes parade solemnly up and down the terrace of the *Trinksaal* with their mugs of lukewarm Baden water. Here, one notices many of the townspeople. For, it must be confessed, comparatively few Germans make the pilgrimage to Baden (where all is decidedly *Luxus*), but the all-year-round inhabitants go in for the waters and the concerts with religious fervour. Must not all – visitors and residents – pay the *Kurtaxe*, and should not one derive one's *Pfennig* worth?

Another method of cure is to seek the solitude of the true *Schwarzwald* – to go to a simple German *Kurhaus*. Here, you will receive rational, careful attention, and you may lose yourself in the heart of the pines where the air is best. But, in this case, you must not look for international elegance, and you must be content with literal rest, far removed from smart clothes, from music and tea-dancing. Your cure companions will be mainly German, with a few Austrians.

But you have followed the line of chic, which is, in this case, also the line of least resistance. The others whom you know, especially Londoners and New Yorkers, have gone, are going, or will go to the famous doctor's famous sanatorium. You join them.

A strange sanatorium, this. A large, solidly built Teuton house, furnished stolidly and without taste or graceful concessions. The air of a hotel, not a hospital. Inside – no busy evidence of nurses. A plain, uncompromising dining-room, set with straight rows of small tables. Men and women dressed for dinner, intent on food bearing numbered porcelain tags. Later – a group sitting on the veranda; a table of bridge; a gradual exodus upstairs to bed; then – ten o'clock, and the *portier* locking the doors with an enormous key, changing into his blue striped jumper, and arranging his mattress for uninterrupted repose.

'Yes, I've lost five kilos. Could have done it at home, I suppose, if I'd had the strength of character. Paris tomorrow – must get some new clothes before I sail. Are you leaving this morning, too?"

VOGUE, March 1929

*Above* 'Obese and lean sit down to dinners of porcelain-tagged foods'
BEATON 1929

*Left* 'And so to bed'
BEATON 1929

*Below* 'A husky maiden sprays a staggering stream on excess pounds'
BEATON 1929

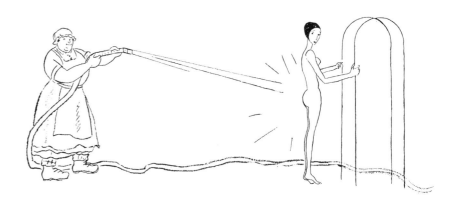

# IN VENICE
## by Noel Coward

"For a few months in every year, a fierce and relentless sun blazes down upon what has been winsomely, if a trifle superficially, described as 'The City of Beautiful Nonsense.' Enthusiastic steam launches forge raucously up and down the Grand Canal, causing perspiring tourists to clutch the carved wooden seats of their gondolas as they bounce up and down in the wash and swirl away from slippery green steps at the precise moment that somebody is attempting to get into them.

Flocks of unembarrassed pigeons are photographed incessantly with a charming disregard of social distinctions, perching upon the more vulnerable anatomical points of minor European royalties and self-conscious American matrons, and, all through the long, scorching days, clouds of effusive superlatives are wafted up and over the shrinking domes and spires of what was once the most graceful and dignified city of the world.

It is not altogether surprising, therefore, that the wealthy exclusive nucleus of cosmopolitans, self-designated as the 'sheik set,' migrates with a slightly uncalled-for air of superiority to the Excelsior Hotel on the Lido. Here, for hours on end, the placid shallows of the long-suffering Adriatic are peppered with bobbing and gesticulating figures. There can be but small consolation for it in the knowledge that it is being ravished by the best people — salt water is a notorious leveller of class differences. Every square inch of fine, powdered sand is churned up by the passing of innumerable toes and dented and depressed by recumbent sun-blistered bodies of various nationalities.

For the benefit of the mercifully unin-itiated, it would, perhaps, be well to describe this Gomorrah of frowzy splendour. An undecorative and incomplete wooden pier wanders listlessly for a few yards into the sea and stops short abruptly, as though discouraged by its own unattractiveness. An amazingly hot strip of sand is semicircularized by two rows of *cabañas*, or bathing huts, intersected by narrow planks that scorch the soles of the feet unless some person has flung down a wet bathing-dress and left a damp patch of grateful coolth. A wider board walk leads from the centre of the beach to a majestic flight of steps culminating in the terrace of the Excelsior Hotel. It is not considered etiquette to penetrate as far as this unless comparatively clothed. Within the lounge, an air of well-ordered civilization soothes the senses — one or two of the bridge players actually seem to be enjoying themselves, unlike their scowling friends on the beach.

The visitors who live in Venice and come out to the Lido only for the day have more chance of ultimate salvation. By the time that they have reached their hotels in the evening and have dressed and dined, the sour lines have been eradicated from their faces and their sanity of outlook is restored. They begin to chatter and laugh again, sublimely unconscious of the pit from which they have escaped. They glide about peacefully in gondolas and watch marionette-like figures jigging about on lantern-hung *Serenatas.* The lights on the Piazza are lazily extinguished. Dim couples wander through the shadows, occasionally speaking Italian — until, at last, for a few hours, the crowd-racked city succumbs to the weary sleep of gently decaying beauty."

VOGUE, September 1926

*Opposite* Santa Maria della Salute BEATON 1932

*Inset* 'The sands of the Adriatic are peppered with the Best People.' Seen on the Lido Beach, *left to right,* Serge Lifar, Countess Edoardo Visconti, Mme Lelong, Prince Jean-Louis de Faucigny-Lucinge, M. de Beistegui, and Princess Jean-Louis de Faucigny-Lucinge 1933

# NEWPORT REIGNS SUPREME

"The word 'exclusive' in its best sense, applies to Newport more, perhaps, than to any other of our resorts. Newport is gay, and it is beautiful, and it is filled with delightful people throughout the season. But it is much more than this. It has the assurance of success – an assurance backed by its history, its traditions, and its background.

Newport was founded in the loveliest of New England locations and became a charming Colonial town. Although it eventually outgrew its original limits and spread along the ocean front, it has always retained its original distinction and this old town, with its dignity and beauty, is still a part of the great charm of Newport, increased, today, by many magnificent houses and fine clubs.

People who have not been there are apt to think that Newport is the great battle-ground of American society. It is, in reality, more comparable to a fortress that newcomers have to storm with patience. And it has a right to this exclusiveness, for it stands for excellence in every thing.

There is no semi-public life in New-port. Only members and their guests can go to the clubs, and the beach is not open to the public. The casual visitor does not see the smart world, except in hasty glimpses of motorcars holding well-dressed women.

The so-called Casino is, in reality, the tennis club, where the championship matches used to be held. This is where the strenuous go in the early morning.

Late in the morning, all the smart world goes to Bailey's Beach. This daily meeting-place has kept the life informal, since it is possible to make all one's plans for the day while mingling with friends on the beach. It is really the heart of the entire colony, yet the same old bath-houses remain. They have had no Urban to create an effect of Eastern splendour, as at the Bath and Tennis Club at Palm Beach. But there are rows of gay parasols on the sand, with low chairs beneath them, some long steamer chairs of brilliant chintz, and chintz backs that give one comfortable support as one sits on the sand.

The variety of costumes worn by the smart women on the beach includes all that is chic for daytime wear. One sees the most suitable of chiffon afternoon dresses, worn with great, soft, flattering hats. These elaborate costumes are seldom seen to-day except at such places as the royal enclosure at Ascot or at Newport on Sunday in August.

At Bailey's Beach, as a rule, the women change their bathing suits quickly after the swim. All types of bathing-suits are worn and almost all the women wear beach coats over the suits, but no stockings. The women do not change from costume to costume, as they do at Palm Beach. In Florida many women change three times each morning – from dress to bathing-suit and then into pyjamas. In connection with this display of fashion, one wit remarked, last winter, 'I have seen hundreds of the most beautiful beach costumes, but not a single wet bathing-suit, except when Tony Biddle got his a little damp, because some one knocked a drink over on him.'

In the last few years, Bailey's Beach has extended its popularity, and now many people lunch on the beach, while every afternoon dozens of lovely children and a good many grown-ups stay for pleasant relaxation. The two golf courses, too, are well filled every afternoon, and, in the late afternoon, there are numberless informal teas, at which bridge is played and often mah jong. This is one of the few places where that game continues to be popular.

At the end of the day, there are dinners – done with absolute perfection. The food is the best in the world, with the possible exception of Paris! There are dancers over every week-end from the middle of July till the first of September.

At the large parties, one notices many Worth and Callot dresses, a good many from Vionnet, and, of course, many from Chanel. Any simple evening dress must be extremely chic.

One is constantly impressed with the meticulous perfection with which the women at Newport are turned out."

VOGUE, September 1927

*Below* At Bailey's Beach, 'really the heart of the entire colony', the smart world sits beneath the shade of parasols to exchange news and make plans MOURGUE 1927

*Right*
VERTES 1937

*Left* 'Against a
Florida fantasy,
here are Lord and
Lady Charles
Cavendish, who
stopped over in
Palm Beach on
their way from
Ireland to
Hollywood.
Although rumour
constantly puts the
former Adèle
Astaire into her
brother Fred's
former films, she
maintains weakly
that she won't
dance'
BEATON 1936

"It's divine—but my husband hates _me_ to wear such low necks"

# PALM BEACH: VILLAGE BY THE SEA
## by Constantin Alajálov

"You probably all know Palm Beach, but I didn't. The sensation that first day at the station of lazy space, rustic and un-rushed, startled me: the low horizon, the flat country, the enormous expansion of sky, the continuous movement of the palms and their heavy shadows. It is a fabulous little village over which you can drive from one end to the other in less than half an hour and across which you can walk in less than ten minutes.

There is a feeling that everything is bleached, buried in violent greenery. The houses, white, pale ochre, washed-out Indian-red, are set in careful gardens, with only a few spots of flowers, and those lack fragrance. The green and blue of water gleam everywhere, with the ocean on one side, the lake on the other. Buzzards fly lazily in the air, and pelicans rush by in military formation.

The pattern of life is well organized, comfortable, polished, *bien soignée*. Patios and pools are the core of outdoor life. Every one gathers, as always, around the private pools splashed with bright coloured cushions and mattresses; men taking sun-baths, women almost never. They never bathe in the ocean and only rarely swim in the pools. They just drop into blue water and, after two or three casual strokes, float exhausted for a few minutes.

The daily round is unalterably loose-textured. People drop in for tennis, a cocktail or two, and stay to lunch outdoors. Dates are vague, and hostesses never know who or how many will be at their tables. Luncheons are therefore informal, noisy, gay.

Faces are natural, relaxed, and the laughter spontaneous. Every one looks better down there, with no trace of tenseness. I liked the casual feeling of life, fresh, lazy, and easy-going. No one bothers to be individual, imaginative. All are doing the same thing, seeing the same people, wearing the same kind of clothes.

In the afternoons, there are backgammon, golf, fishing, polo. People at polo spread blankets on the ground and look like bits from the paintings of Raoul Dufy. Nights they go dancing in the moonlight, sometimes to The Patio, sometimes to the Colony: a Venetian carnival with familiar faces growing unfamiliar.

Sometimes they're off to the wrestling bouts on Mondays at Lake Worth to watch 'Sailor' Jack Adams. Sometimes to Bradley's, to the small circular hall caught up in half-darkness, where the light is all thrown on the game tables. Five or six attendants in black surround each table, more of them are at the entrance, more behind each column. There's a feeling of being watched constantly. Why do people gamble with such lack of gaiety and enthusiasm . . . with such solemnity? The impression is of darkness, tall columns, attendants, silence, bright-green tables, jewelled wrists . . .

More Palm Beach impressions: Mrs Harrison Williams in her pink bathing-suit with a white bathing-cap — like a tropical flower floating in blue water. The sophistication of Adèle Cavendish — formerly Astaire — with her enchanting sensation of out-of-placeness in the tropical outdoors, her high heels, and cute, complicated white hat."

VOGUE, March 1936

*Left* The sun shines, and the smart world relaxes – while Nana, 'British to the heel,' in flowing veil and crisp uniform, minds the 'brood of babies'
WILLAUMEZ 1933

*Below* Four in the morning at Mrs Harrison Williams' party
ALAJALOV 1933

# PALM BEACH

"Before you can capture the momentary rhythm of this loveliest of resorts and understand the whys of what the smart world does, where it goes, and what it wears, you must know that, this year, Palm Beach is different. There is a wholesale reversion to a more casual and simple life. True, the people, in most instances, are the same ones who were here before, but, this year, the simple background throws interesting personalities into bolder relief. No one is trying to live up to a delusion of grandeur and pomposity.

And what does this more agreeable living actually mean? Rising early – that is, fairly early – in the morning seems to be one of the first developments, if you are energetic – and almost every one is. Then off to some one's tennis-court, clad either in a bathing-suit, or in one of the new shorts-and-shirt costumes that are rapidly supplanting tennis dresses. After a few good broiling sets, a plunge in the near-by pool follows. At the Bath and Tennis Club, you change to shorts or pyjamas in the *cabaña* after the dip.

This new fashion of wearing short-trousered costumes, which has come to us by way of the Lido and Antibes, is typical of the 1930 type. These costumes have been adopted because of their usefulness, rather than for effect."

VOGUE, March 1930

*Left* Mrs Harrison Williams
BEATON 1934

*Top* The new Palm Beach Bath and Tennis Club
BOLIN 1927

*Centre* Little Gloria Vanderbilt, with her mother, Mrs Raymond T. Baker 1924

*Right* Addison Mizner, architect of Palm Beach
BEATON 1931

# UNDER THE SUN

"When the first woman with the first cultivated coat of tan made her appearance upon the Riviera, the smart world looked up and remarked to itself, 'Here is something new under the sun.' And it has been proceeding on this principle ever since!

From a chic note, sunburn became a trend, then an established fashion, and now the entire feminine world is sunburn conscious! But merely to be sunburned is not to be chic, and therein lies the crux of this whole sunburn situation. One has to be sunburned smartly, and, to be so, one must needs make a serious business of it, first of acquiring it, then of dressing for it. And those who don't recognize the importance of this credo are apt to be more sunburned than they are smart.

As the sunburn movement has gathered momentum, it has gained for itself a whole series of attributes – sunburn frocks, sunburn suits, sunburn cosmetics, sunburn lingerie. It has established its own range of colours. It has decreed its own scheme of make-up. It has even gone so far as to determine the back-lines of entire summer wardrobes, as can be seen in the costumes that appear below. And failure awaits the neophyte who 'goes sunburn' without knowing these rules, or the hardened burner who knows, but disregards.

The first important step in sunburn is the way in which it is acquired. To-day there are many preparations available that actually eliminate the painful stage. Such a preparation may take the form of a cream or a lotion or oil (there are dependable versions of all these forms upon the market), but, whatever it is, it must be applied carefully on every part of the body that is to be exposed to the sun's rays. When one is on the beach, this protective covering should not only be used before one faces the sun, but be renewed after going in the water.

The foundation of a tan is usually acquired upon the beach, and thus the bathing-suit should provide the lines of demarcation for all costumes. This is a backless age, and there is no single smarter sunburn gesture than to have every low-backed costume cut on exactly the same lines, so that each one makes a perfect frame for a smooth, brown back. Bathing-suits, beach pyjamas, tennis dresses, and evening frocks, all may descend as low as they like, providing that they descend to the same depth together.

VOGUE, July 1929

*Opposite* 'The hand-knit suit swims into fashion': bathing suits and beach clothes for the *'monde qui s'amuse'*. The sailcloth backless overall, *left,* is modelled by Lee Miller, who was to become an acclaimed photographer and war-correspondent HOYNINGEN-HEUNE 1930

*Left* 'The beautifully-sunbrowned backless mode' HARRIET MESEROLE 1929

# OUR LIVES ON THE RIVIERA

*Above left* Lady Mendl, 'airily poised on the shoulder of her instructor in her gardens at Antibes'
LUCIEN EYSSERIE 1928

*Above right* Three well-known figures relax on the water: Amy Mollison, intrepid flyer; Randolph Churchill, politician; Clare Boothe Luce, writer
1936

*Opposite* The dress for a Riviera night: a 'billowy frock', by Chanel, with the perfect uncovered back
ERIC 1933

"*Vogue* discovered the summer Riviera six years ago when we first went to the tiny casino at Juan-les-Pins, where there were only a handful of people, and put up at the half-closed Hotel Majestic at Cannes in the month of August. But when we prophesied the future of this summer playground, little did we know that our dream would so rapidly turn into reality – a reality that now completely surpasses our most optimistic predictions.

Juan-les-Pins used to be a sleepy village, closed up tight at mid-day. At the bathing-rocks at Antibes there was only a tiny pavilion, but this has since grown into one of the most elaborate bathing casinos in the world. Six years ago Cannes, too, resembled a winter resort enveloped, for the summer, in slip covers, with only a few of the local shops and one hotel open. Now the place is teeming with life in summer, far more so than in winter. The harbour is filled with yachts and speed-boats, and the Croisette bristles with the branches of well-known Paris houses – dressmakers, jewellers, and what-not. At every other step there is a bar or an out-door terrace, where people dine at night in the light of shaded candles. A ceaseless procession of motor-cars and people promenading on foot goes by. But, unlike the first two or three seasons during which the Riviera was becoming fashionable in summer, the country has spread out, so to speak, until now there are groups of people all along the coast for miles, from Cap-Martin to Toulon.

At Deauville, Biarritz, Venice, or any of the other famous seaside resorts, the whole world can be seen at one hour of the day at some particular rendezvous. But on the Riviera, one would have to have an auto-giro and spend most of one's time in the air, to keep up with the active life of the different sets of people, scattered as they are now. It has become a fairground, bordering an endless road of countless curves along the sea, and is almost the most amusing place we know."

VOGUE, September 1931

*Right* Lunching in the Casino at Cannes
ERIC 1931

*Left* 'The fronds of the palm tree, the curl of her hair, the curl of the chair — they all contribute to the effective picture that Lady Abdy makes in her new Provençal peasant sun-hat of natural straw. This beautiful lady is Russian by birth and exercises great influence on fashion in Paris. Because she wears this hat, all smart women on the Riviera will do so, too'
HOYNINGEN-HEUNE 1932

# RIVIERA DAYS

"They say you will eventually see all the richest people, all the most famous people, all the most fashionable people, lunching in the Casino at Cannes. Certainly you will see strange people, hunched figures wearing fortunes in emeralds, and a few well-dressed women. There are any number of dowdies, too, and more grey heads than there are blondes — for Cannes is not as young as it looks. It takes a good part of a lifetime to amass all the jewels you see.
VOGUE, month 1931

*Above* On the maiden voyage of the *Normandie*: 'Lanvin's Italian red cape and Schiaparelli's etched satin dress' ERIC 1935

*Opposite* Relaxing on the S.S. *President Hoover* – 'luxurious new ship of the Dollar Steamship Lines, which goes to Manila by way of Havana, San Francisco, Shanghai and other fascinating ports' ANTON BRUEHL 1931

# MAIDEN VOYAGE OF THE NORMANDIE
## by Lee Creelman (wife of the artist, 'Eric')

"A lovely name, *Normandie*. Perhaps that is one reason that the maiden voyage of the great ship has made such an appeal to the world's imagination.

As the ship moved slowly out of the harbour, we saw that the piers and shores of Havre were black with people massed in immense crowds. Airplanes played about the ship like winged dolphins. The deep voice of the *Normandie* roared farewell, the crowds roared back – and we were on our way.

Passengers coming aboard at Southampton said that thousands had waited there for hours, and were rewarded with a magnificent spectacle as she came in sight. The indirect lighting on her colossal funnels, and her name blazoned in enormous letters on the sun-deck made her look like a ship of fire.

The vast salon with its black and gold tapestry, its beautiful Aubusson chairs and carpets; the bar with its immense gold lacquer decorations by Jean Dunand, its curtains in the new *velours Normandie* by Colcombet; the golden staircase leading to the grill – are magnificent, but indescribable. As one enters the grill, a great circular room with enormous windows facing the sea, one realizes, almost for the first time, that this is really a ship. Looking back over the ocean, barred as far as one can see by the wake of the sea-monster, the speed seemed incredible.

The grill-room opened on the second night at midnight and immediately became the most popular room on the ship. Perhaps the most beautiful night-club in the world, the Normandie Grill is destined to become famous. After a late supper and dancing, to watch the dawn come up over the sea, through the great windows which surround the room, is an unforgettable experience.

An amazing conception of a room, strange, mysterious, the immense dining-hall is like a great crystal cavern lighted by luminous stalactites.

Behind all this golden magnificence lies a story of courage in these difficult times. The *Normandie* is a symbol of the arts and crafts, the industry of a great nation. France has made a brave and splendid gesture towards the return of commerce and the pursuits of peace."

VOGUE, July 1935

# FIRST IMPRESSIONS –
# MAIDEN VOYAGE OF THE QUEEN MARY
## by Cecil Beaton

*Opposite page: above,* on the sun deck – passengers at one of their favourite occupations; *below right* Passengers fight fat in the super-gymnasium; *below left* High dives in the swimming pool
BEATON 1936

"There must always be a certain amount of chaos on a maiden voyage. It is not expected that the service will be good, for the first trip is like the first night of some gigantic stage production. It is said that on the *Queen Mary* calm and comfort were enjoyed in comparison with other first voyages.

When constructing a boat, even a luxury liner, the English do not consider their women very carefully. There are hardly any large mirrors in the general rooms, no great flight of stairs for ladies to make an entrance. The decorations have a monotony without uniformity; there is too much woodwork. The effort at being modern is decidedly forced. The Verandah Grill, however, is by far the prettiest room on any ship – becomingly lit, gay in colour and obviously so successful that it would be crowded if twice its present size. The cabins are beautifully equipped and more refreshingly decorated than on any other boat.

The approach to New York was historic and deeply moving. Aeroplanes roared past the portholes of the cabins. A Versailles *grands eaux* effect was produced by the fountains of fire boats. From every window kisses were blown and handkerchiefs waved. Along the Battery, the crowds had been standing since daylight, forty deep. New York, most appreciative of all achievement, gave a magnificent welcome to the *Queen Mary*."

VOGUE, July 1936

*Right* In Egypt: The Countess Pecci-Blunt in front of one of the Great Pyramids at Giza 1929

*Below* Among the dunes of the Sahara: the time for prayer
SAALBERG 1926

# WHERE EAST MEETS WEST

"Practically every single time that Schiaparelli buys a railway ticket, there are fruitful consequences for this world of ours. Last year, it was Russia and the Soviet comrades. This year – Tunisia. With her daughter, Gogo, she spent part of the summer there – where the African moon rises like a red-hot pancake over the Mediterranean, the countryside is dipped in the scent of orange-blossoms, the frightening desert is a back-drop, and the world is all Arabs, Berbers, Moors, Bedouins, and Tuaregs.

Luck was with Schiaparelli. Even the forbidden private wing of one of the great aristocratic Arab houses was opened to her, and her veiled hostesses, as one woman to another, tried on for her all their ceremonial costumes. One even wore, in her honour, a bride's dress of pure gold, stiff as armour, and shoes of beaten silver with two-inch soles dangling with amulets.

At another more emancipated

Arabian house, after a feast of mutton skewered on a sword, her host brought in — not Bedouin dancing-girls — but Bedouin sewing-girls, to unravel the mysteries of Oriental sewing, draping, and veil twisting.

But it's the men's clothes, Schiaparelli thinks, that are richest in colour. This is still a male continent, made for men, for hardship and endeavour, yet the men — startling as the paradox is to us — put flowers behind their ears and sleep in lace-decorated bedrooms. Trunk after trunk of their clothes went back to Paris with Schiaparelli — full of strange breeches and embroidered shirts, the suavely wrapped turbans and enormous hats, pompon-rimmed. Those fantastic skirt-pants of the Tuareg tribe who, legend says, descended from Crusaders who got off the beaten track. The crudely dyed silks and anything but crudely woven fabrics — some as gauzy as clouds. The barbaric belts and jewellery. Probably every button in Tunisia is stamped on Schiaparelli's subconscious — and may soon be stamped on ours."

VOGUE, August 1936

*Above* In Syria: the ruined Roman temple at Baalbek
SAALBERG 1926

*Above left* Schiaparelli *(left)* tries on a Bedouin headdress, under expert instruction
HORST 1936

*Left* Bon Voyage
PAGES 1938

*Right* In Arabian
sands
MOURGUE 1931

*Overleaf* The Port
Washington
Airport,
fashionable
travellers watch
the Bermuda
Clipper Ship taxi
up in travel suits as
elegant and up-to-
the-minute as their
chosen form of
transport
WILLAUMEZ 1937

Including WINTER TRAVEL Features

# THE SPORTING LIFE

'When I go cub-hunting, ought I to take my groom with me, and does he wear livery?'
'No.'

VOGUE, November 1931

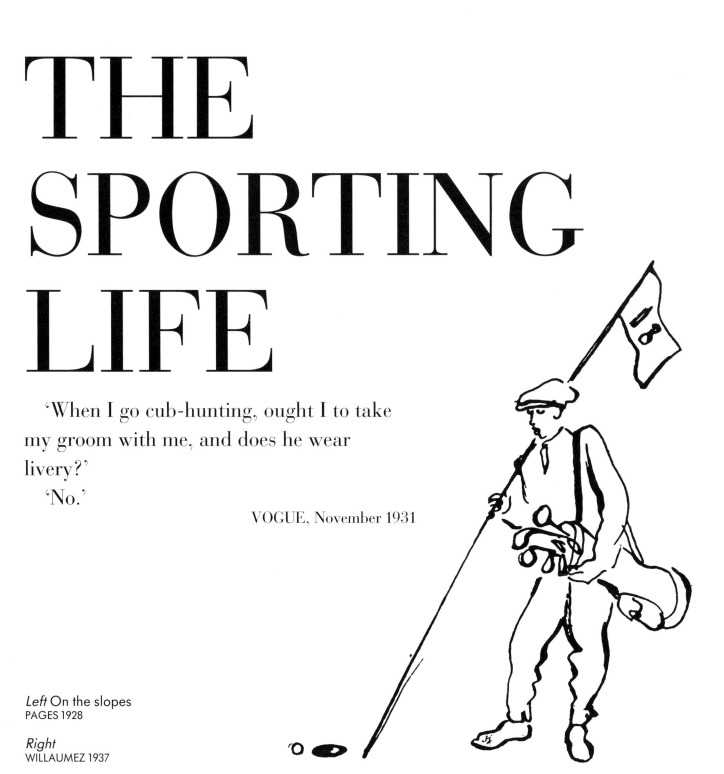

*Left* On the slopes
PAGES 1928

*Right*
WILLAUMEZ 1937

When *Vogue* first appeared, in the era before the Great War, active sports were still regarded as a largely masculine preserve. Some society women might follow the guns at a shooting-party, play croquet or golf in cumbersome skirts, or ride to hounds, side-saddle; but for most Edwardian elegantes, an interest in sport was confined to appearing, fashionably dressed, at race meetings, and attending the Season's polo matches and tennis tournaments. In the aftermath of the First World War, however, attitudes began to change. Women who had donned overalls and uniforms to drive ambulances or run canteens were no longer content with a life of corseted inactivity; and by the mid-1920s, the pages of *Vogue* were filled with images of society sportswomen, riding in point-to-points, racing down ski-slopes, and taking to the skies at the controls of their own aeroplanes.

Dispensing with a chauffeur to drive oneself became a new hallmark of chic. 'Women Who Once Drove Because of Patriotism, Now Continue For Enjoyment', declared a 1922 *Vogue* headline, beside a page of photographs of Lady Diana Cooper posing in her smart two-seater convertible, and Mrs Belmont Tiffany 'at the wheel of her Studebaker runabout'. As an admiring caption to one motoring feature, 'Seen At The Steering-Wheel', put it, 'Lady Chesham is well known for her interest in sports, and she drives as well as she rides.'

Those who rode in the 1920s and '30s did so with a new freedom. While some kept up the side-saddle tradition, others, dressed in well-cut breeches, now hunted astride, played polo, and took part in steeplechases (earning the half-admiring, half-patronising epithet, 'Hell-for-Leather Girls' from one 1937 contributor). Advice on the correct form for hunting clothes (and etiquette) appeared regularly in the magazine; and the thoroughbred beauty of such well-known horsewomen as Lady Avice Spicer and Mrs Harold E. Talbott provided inspiration for some of *Vogue*'s greatest photographers.

*Above* The French tennis champion, Miss Suzanne Lenglen, in an 'ideal tennis dress' by Jean Patou 1927

*Below* Racing at Belmont 1929

In the fashion world, the 'sports mode' became an all-pervasive influence. The look of the era was lean, short-skirted and energetic; led by the great Chanel, chic women from Paris to Palm Beach appeared in simple jersey dresses and mannish tweeds, golfing cardigans and tailored slacks. For actual sports clothes, *Vogue* presented ever more enticing possibilities – from the svelte silk tennis dresses of Jean Patou, to brief knitted bathing suits, suede riding breeches, and jazzy Deco golf sweaters. Skiing required a specially imaginative wardrobe. By day, one might appear on the slopes, like Lady Abdy, in little woollen shorts over leggings; or like Mrs Michael Arlen, in trim plus-fours; but by night, at St Moritz or Kitzbühel, 'society's butterflies' emerged in silk dresses, with furs and jewels – looking none the less exotic for the addition of practical rubber boots.

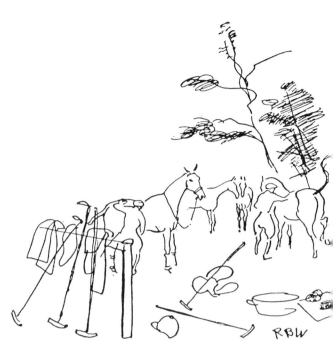

WILLAUMEZ 1937

Femininity had to be maintained, even on the sportsfield: the object was to join the men at their own games, not beat them. Playing polo, in boyish breeches, Lady Diana Cooper shaded her fair face under a becoming hat; on the tennis court, Mrs Harrison Williams protected her well-coiffed hair with a neat bandeau. Features on the sporting heroines of the day – such as the tennis stars Suzanne Lenglen and Helen Wills Moody, and the flying pioneer Amelia Earhart – invariably stressed their fashion sense and feminine appeal. Would-be sportswomen who appeared unfit, ill-dressed, or out of place, were ready targets for *Vogue*'s cartoonists – as were those aspiring sports*men* who appeared on the grouse-moors in fancy-dress kilts.

Shooting and fishing remained, according to *Vogue*'s contributors, essentially masculine preoccupations. There were women who joined the guns with enthusiasm and shot with expertise – usually after 'hours of practice . . . under the skilled (and stern) tuition of the family gamekeeper', as *Vogue* put it. But shooting-parties were generally mentioned in tones of humorous resignation, with wry references to the discomforts of muddy fields and badly-plumbed Scottish castles. The new-found pleasures of sport – like most of society's diversions – were best enjoyed in fashionable surroundings; and for *Vogue*'s readers in the 1920s and '30s, the tennis-courts of the Riviera, the 'winter playground' of St Moritz and the golf-courses of Le Touquet offered the ideal settings for the sporting life.

# OUR LIVES ABOVE THE SNOWLINE
## St Moritz Notes

"Of all the resorts of our day, the most up-to-date arena of the moderns is Saint Moritz. To the next generation, Saint Moritz will probably be the background of the legend about this one, just as Homburg and Monte Carlo were the backgrounds for the legend of the generation that went before. The people who have never been to Saint Moritz think of it as the one place they intend to visit, and those who have the habit of going there never miss a season.

In its own way, Saint Moritz presents a show, too, but it is typical of our generation rather than the Edwardians – a show that is not all 'on the back,' so to speak. There are more dogs and personal servants at the Palace Hotel, nurses, children, governesses, and what-not, than one sees at most places to-day. But you feel, rather than see, the expensive atmosphere. And this is characteristic of our day, because 'show' is no longer the fashion. The world is always 'snob,' but every generation is 'snob' about different things, and ours is 'snob' about amusing personalities, people who do things, more than anything else. Therefore, you have this set at Saint Moritz leading an up-to-date life of sports and elegance.

All day long, they are out in the snow, skiing on the mountains, skating, bobbing, or sleighing, with half the world looking on at the other half, the serious sports. Hardly any one is to be found at the hotel at lunch time, because the new ski-club at the top of the second funic-

ular, which climbs to Corviglia two thousand feet above Saint Moritz, is the mecca for every one.

In the evening, around ten o'clock, the atmosphere of the hotel suddenly changes, and the booted and be-trousered ladies appear very much dressed up and wearing all their jewels. (Of course, this is no more true of Saint Moritz than anywhere else, since all the chic internationals are dressed up every night of their lives, no matter where they are, and they always wear all their jewels – another modern idea.)"

VOGUE, January 1932

*Left* The future King Edward VIII when Prince of Wales, skiing at Kitzbühel. 'It was *Vogue* who discovered Kitzbühel and announced it to the world, since when it has become the fashionable skiing centre of all Europe'
1935

*Opposite* Mrs Joseph Kennedy, wife of the US Ambassador in London, on the ski slopes with two of her children, Jean and Teddy
1939

*Right* 'In the evening at Saint Moritz the most strenuous sportswomen turn to brilliant butterflies. Lady Westmoreland, left, wears a gown of red velvet with inserts of red chiffon, and carries a wrap of leopard bordered with black fox. Both she and her sable-cloaked companion wear the high boots that are a necessity, even in the evening, if one goes out into the cold air'
MOURGUE 1926

*Right* The smart set
1937

*Opposite* Miss Enid Riddle, accompanied by the Venetian artist Tollentino, who is enjoying 'the absolutely thrilling sport known as Skijoring'. Miss Riddle wears 'daring leather riding breeches' with a belted woollen sweater REHBINDER 1924

*Left* 'The Comtesse de Beaumont, a very chic woman and a great winter sports enthusiast, is here seen against a decorative and appropriate background of snow-covered trees. She is wearing a skiing costume under her mink coat' HOYNINGEN-HEUNE 1931

'For the beginner, the first day is a depressing business. Everything is accompanied by shouts and roars from the teacher, and one wonders how much longer the seat of one's pants will last . . . Perhaps this is why one learns so quickly'
WILLAUMEZ 1936

# THE SHOOTING PARTY
## by The Hon Nancy Mitford

". . . It is curious that, while most men pretend to like shooting, it brings their worst passions to the surface, especially when they are getting ready to leave the house after breakfast. If you wish to be really tactful, stay in bed until quite twelve o'clock. You will be obliged to go out to lunch with the guns and spend the afternoon with them, so put on your stoutest tweeds (choosing a colour that will not shock the birds), thick shoes, and a mackintosh.

On arriving at the appointed place for lunch, which will be either, if you are lucky, a warm room in some cottage, or, more probably, a windswept haystack, you will certainly have to wait for at least an hour. When at last the men appear, do not speak to them until they have addressed you first. If the shooting has been good they will come up to you smiling, saying something like 'Well, well, this isn't the worst part of the day is it, what? Ha, ha, what?' and conversation will flow smoothly. If it has been bad the tactful woman remains silent until the softening influence of food and drink has been felt.

After luncheon you will accompany the guns to some bleak hedgerow, where you will sit quite still for a great time in silence. If you must speak, avoid remarks like 'Please don't beat poor Fido quite so hard.' When the man with whom you are standing breaks a heavy silence by saying angrily, 'Shut up and lie down', remember that he is probably addressing not you, but his dog.

At the end of each drive you will be expected to wander about with your eyes fixed on the ground, pretending to look for dead birds. The fact that even if you should happen to find one, no bribe would induce you to touch it, will probably render your search of but small value, but it is better to appear happy and occupied for fear that your hostess should think that you are bored. It is a consolation during this time to remember that no afternoon lasts for ever.

That evening at dinner, conversation will present no difficulties. You will be completely neglected by the men, who will shout at each other across the table: 'That was a high bird down by King's Cover.'

'Your dog better now? I knew Elliman's would do the trick.'

When, after two or three days of this sort of thing, you arrive back at your home, you will appreciate the feeling that, in spite of being a woman, you do count for something there. Your writing-table will seem particularly comfortable as you sit down to accept two more shooting invitations which you find waiting in the hall on your return."

VOGUE, December 1929

*Right* 'Shooting is a ravenous passion'
VERTES 1935

*Below* 'Country make-up should vary as much from town make-up as daytime does from evening'
WILLAUMEZ 1930

# OUR LIVES WITH GUNS AND DOGS

"And so the shooting season. And very nice too. Sun on the stubble fields, dew on the thorn, small brown partridges whirring across a fence. Nice smells — wood smoke and loam and tweeds and burnt-out cartridges. Nice dogs — black labradors with treacly eyes, brown spaniels with untidy feet. Nice lunches — hot-pot and baked potatoes and jam-puffs, on trestle tables in keepers' cottages and farmhouse parlours.

It's not so long since women merely skimmed the cream off days like these. Made first appearance just in time for lunch, made conversation to the 'guns' for one drive afterwards, made tracks for home in more than easy time for tea, taking little more than just a passing interest in the whole day's sport.

Now the form is very different. Go to practically any shooting-party and you'll find the women up and out almost as early as the men, armed with enthusiasm and shooting-sticks; hobnailed, hatless, and entirely happy. Nor is it rare to find them taking even more active part. Joining the guns in actual fact by being one of them. Taking a stand on every drive (complete with dog and loader) and shooting all through the day with tireless energy, and no mean skill — result of serious concentration in shooting-schools, and hours of practice 'potting' rabbits or clay pigeons, under the skilled (and stern) tuition of the family gamekeeper . . .

But whether out to shoot or watch, there's not much argument about the fun of being out, in this 'season of mists and mellow fruitfulness,' of turning leaves and crisp autumnal days."

VOGUE October 1938

*Above* 'Lady Bowden plays the woman's part to perfection in an English shooting-party by admiring the bag. Lord Wimborne, Sir Harold Bowden and Lord Savile are included in the group' 1929

*Right* 'Many women prefer to hunt side-saddle'. Part of the field at the Garth meet 1922

*Below* 'The Duke of Marlborough with his sons, Lord Blandford *right* and Lord Ivor Spencer-Churchill' 1925

*Opposite* The future King George VI at the opening meet of the Pytchley Hounds 1928

# THE SIDE-SADDLE HABIT
## by Katharine St George

"If her appointments are perfect, if she's a skilled rider, a woman in a side-saddle is a joy to the eyes.

Many women prefer to hunt in a side-saddle – because it is more comfortable for long hours in the hunting-field, because it gives a securer seat, because women's knee-structure is naturally unsuited to riding astride and because they look better in a side-saddle.

If you ride side-saddle, the question of appointments is all-important, beginning, logically, with underclothes. Most comfortable are the silk-and-wool vest and pants, with the pants cut long enough to fit well over the knees.

The stock is often a stumbling-block. However, if you'll study the elaborate descriptions and pictures that are usually enclosed with the stocks sent to you by any good shirtmaker, you will come near enough. It is not necessary for your stock to look exactly like the one on the tailor's dummy, but it must be neat and stay in place during a long day's hunting.

Go to the best tailor you know for your riding habit, and have it fitted until it is absolutely right. If you take your own saddle when having the skirt fitted, the result is bound to be more satisfactory.

When hunting in full dress – which you'll do most of the time, after the cubbing season is over – you'll wear your habit with hunt collar and buttons, and always your silk hat. With a topper, wear a veil and bun. Veils add much to the smartness of your appearance, and protect you from low-hanging branches and bushes. Hair should be as close to the head as possible, and lashed down with a net. On the hunting-field, everything should be trim and clean-cut. Make-up should be eliminated entirely or used very sparingly.

Next to the horse itself, the saddle is the most important item. At the beginning of each hunting-season, the saddler should make sure paddings and linings are in good shape. If you have a new horse, it's a good idea to try the saddle on him and let the saddler make any necessary adjustments. A side-saddle shouldn't result in a sore back for the horse.

The horse, of course, is the main thing. A woman who hunts needs to be beautifully mounted – particularly if she's hunting side-saddle. First, it's harder for a horse carrying a side-saddle to jump. Second, you're likely to go under the horse if you get a fall. So your horse should be big, fast, well-mannered. Manners, in fact, are the great essential for your horse and you."

VOGUE, December 1938

*Left* A keen
horsewoman, Mrs
Van Alen was Miss
Eleanor Langley of
New York and
Westbury, before
her marriage
STEICHEN 1929

*Right* Lady Avice
Spicer, wife of
Captain Frank
Spicer MFH, joint
master of the
Beaufort hounds
RAWLINGS 1936

*Above* 'As the scarlet postilions come trotting down the course a roar goes up from the crowd, Their Majesties and their guests speed by on their way to the Royal Box, and the race meeting begins'
1934

*Left* Racing at Belmont
WILLAUMEZ 1935

Right Summer racing days
ERIC 1933

**LA MODE
DE PRINTEMPS**

AVRIL 1933
PRIX 6 FRANCS
LES ÉDITIONS CONDÉ NAST

PREMIERS MODÈLES D'HIVE
LES CHAPEAU
SEPTEMBRE 193
PRIX 10 FRANC

REVUE MENSUELLE. LES ÉDITIONS CONDÉ NA

# AT THE RACES

"To any one who has never before been to Ascot, it is, out of all the London season, the great adventure. Every English man or woman who has a right to a card – the English get cards by applying to the Court Chamberlain – goes at least once in his lifetime to Ascot, the greatest race-meet of the year in England, where the best horses are run. Being in the Royal Enclosure at Ascot is being on the inside looking out. 'Distinguished foreigners' apply through their own embassies for enclosure tickets, and every one wears his badge conspicuously pinned to his coat lapel or wrap. Impressive-looking attendants in green plush liveries stand at the various entrances to the Royal Enclosure to watch with hawk-like eyes and prevent any one without a badge from passing the iron railings. Few people have ever fooled the green plush guards.

Within the Enclosure to-day, one sees the finest looking collection of men and women that it is possible to see. The men are all magnificent in their grey toppers, light trousers and waistcoats, and their smart ties (no one wears spats). As an American said, 'This is the only country left where the men are the birds of plumage.' All the women we know at Ascot are very well dressed, in print dresses under thin summer coats, and in both large and small hats. But Ascot is famous for big 'laughs' in the way of incredible clothes that must have taken the whole year to think out and that make the mannequins at the Paris races look tame by comparison. Most of these incredible-looking ladies are only to be seen in the paddock, and I have never yet discovered who they are or where they come from."

VOGUE, June 1935

*Left* The smart crowd 'who gather round the chestnut tree in the paddock at Longchamp'
WILLAUMEZ 1934

*Opposite* Winning colours
ERIC 1938

*Right* Not in Dublin, surprisingly, but in the back streets of Chantilly: Jack McCann's Bar, a 'favourite gathering place of men whose lives are devoted to the care of horses'
ERIC 1931

*Below* Over the sticks
PAGES 1930

# AN IRISH BAR – IN CHANTILLY

"Jack McCann's Bar, tucked into one of the back streets of Chantilly, is a New-market transplanted to France – the favourite gathering place for men whose lives are devoted to the care of horses. Old men, slight but still bright, gather here to reminisce on their once-brilliant past as jockeys . . . Jack acts as book-maker; serves the drinks; and when he is in the mood, he will regale you with stories about famous races, famous jockeys and famous horses. If he likes you, he may whisper in your ear a tip on the next day's winner."

VOGUE, October 1931

# POLO –
# 'THE GALLOPING
# GAME'

"Every year the popularity of polo seems to be increasing. Nor is this a matter for surprise, because there is no field sport so delightful to play or so fascinating to follow as the galloping game. A big afternoon at one of the polo clubs presents a scene of brilliancy and animation not readily to be forgotten. All that is best in sport and society appears to be grouped around the polo ground, and excitement is intense as two beautifully-mounted teams fight out the issue chukker by chukker.

One of the most interesting and eventful polo seasons since the end of the War is now starting. Its chief feature will be the building up of a team which is to be sent to the United States in the hope of winning back the International Cup. This trophy was captured by America three years ago, but it is believed that England will be able to put a stronger side into the field than was available on that occasion. It is taking this country a long time to recover from the set-back which the War inevitably caused in the polo world, but there are welcome signs that we are regaining our former strength.

The Prince of Wales was the first to offer to lend his stud of ponies for the use of the English team, and his example has been followed by a number of the most famous players, with the result that our men should be well mounted in the matches at Meadowbrook. The Prince is passionately devoted to the game, and has certainly improved appreciably in form in recent seasons."

VOGUE, May 1924

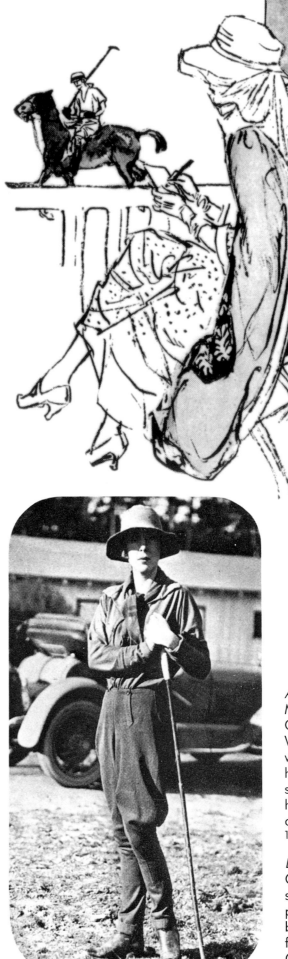

*Above left* 'At the Meadowbrook Club, Mrs J. Watson Webb watches her husband's long shots from under her hat of white organdie'
1920

*Left* 'Lady Diana Cooper was snapped in her polo costume just before leaving the field at Del Monte, California'
1927

*Left* Helen Wills Moody. One of the most stylish and popular of all America's women tennis stars, she also painted, wrote and appeared on lecture tours.
HORST 1938

*Opposite* The Prince and Princess de Faucigny-Lucinge on the small golf course at Le Touquet
1924

*Below* 'This is smart little Alyse de B. . . who is enjoying her first social and sports season. The amount of sod removed by this inexpert *ingénue* is amazing, but all is forgiven by the enamoured Greens Committee'
FISH 1928

# TENNIS TALK
## by Mrs Satterthwaite

"Even the most conservative-minded are now giving up the idea that lawn tennis is too strenuous a pursuit for women, since we have so many proofs that it is possible to play it marvellously and at the same time look pretty and be perfectly fit. The most anxious mother need not be afraid of her daughter contracting a 'tennis face,' with muscles set into a dreadful frown of concentration.

No one can look more utterly determined, if it comes to that, than Miss Helen Wills, but her face always preserves its unruffled serenity. She has gained in good looks and poise in the last four years just as she has strengthened and improved her game, and gives the impression of having much more in reserve than she had in 1924.

This young champion is, in fact, a perfect pattern for any girl to emulate. Her game is like herself, straightforward and honest, no subleties or 'trick' shots, just forceful strokes well executed and produced. Her dresses are in the same spirit as her play – nothing for show, but everything for expediency and comfort on the court. Some people consider her clothes too simple, but Miss Wills would never have occupied the unique position in women's tennis that she does to-day if she thought of tennis in terms of such things as smart ensembles, coloured sweaters, bandeaux and handkerchiefs. To her the game means so much that all the lesser adjuncts are the merest trifles.

One very noticeable thing about our girl champions at Wimbledon is their grace, distinctly the reverse of what some people have prophesied – that hard exercise and strain would thicken the ankles, coarsen the complexion, and lead to general ungainliness."

VOGUE, June 1929

# GOLF TALK

"Golf is *the* week-end sport. To one who muses on the great and growing popularity of this game, the following thoughts inevitably occur: that it is surprisingly well adapted to both old and young: that it is the greatest boon to the hostess in occupying and entertaining the week-end guest; that it is admirable for pairing-off couples with matrimonial prospects in a discreetly casual manner; that it gives men unexampled opportunities for the exercise of imagination in their attire; that most women look well in the kind of clothes that are suitable for golf; that the golf umbrellas in black and yellow checks or red plaids are alone worth the game. The one drawback is a weighty one: it lies in the frightful liability to 'golf-talk' to which every player is exposed."

VOGUE, October 1930

*Below* 'For the stylish stout, nothing could be more chic than this jumper and skirt worn by Mrs Carrie Muchmore. The material, extra wide, is in soft tones which blend with the landscape'
FISH 1928

# SHE FLIES HER OWN

"Learning to fly is both a stimulating and a nerve-racking business. To begin with, not only do you fly, but you go to ground school, where you study things like engines, aerodynamics, navigation, meteorology, and – of all things – traffic regulations. And besides that, there are flights with your instructor – flights that bring out the best and the worst in you.

It takes you, if you are an average beginner, about ten flights with an instructor before you can solo – and during them you are equipped with earphones, but your instructor is not. Consequently, when he makes remarks on your mental capacities there is nothing for you to do but listen. If he puts you into a spin with instructions to pull the plane out, and your mind suddenly becomes a blank (which it is nearly certain to do the first time this happens to you) – if you forget that you must neutralize the controls – if you forget everything except that it was a great pity you ever took up flying – it is fairly exasperating to have him remark acidly, 'I have children if you haven't,' and pull the plane out. But it is maddening – and very good for you – to have to save your retort until twenty minutes later, on the ground.

But when at last you do fly solo – what an indescribable feeling it is! To landlubbers, the most astonishing reaction is the flier's lack of fear. Nervous you are, of course, but thrilled, even exalted. It's the moment you've been looking forward to for weeks, perhaps months. You and the ship are a part of each other – freed from the bonds of earth – consuming space with wings, a motor, and your own mind.

Whether you prefer an open or a closed plane is almost impossible to decide: the two fill such different needs. Every one agrees that an open ship is twice as exhilarating, but, for the cold months and for long trips, a closed plane is obviously more practical.

One thing, however, is indispensable in an open plane, and that is a helmet, to keep out the noise and to keep in your hair. A white canvas one, like Mrs Lindbergh's, is good for the South, and a leather for the north. For long trips, Mrs Lindbergh wears jodhpurs and a double-breasted leather jacket from Abercrombie and Fitch. Miss Earhart wears the same sort of clothes, except that her jacket is of lighter weight.

As for parachutes, some women fliers wear them, some do not; but most fliers agree that, in cross-country flights or in stunting, it is wise to do so. A parachute weighs eighteen pounds and is awkward, but there are times when to leave it off is merely foolhardy. Mrs. James P. Mills (the former Alice du Pont), who flew to South America with her brother, following the route of the Pan-American Airlines, wears a parachute. As she puts it: "I think you can fly *in a conservative way* and fly a great deal, with no fear of danger."

There is one question in flying that is highly debatable (and debated). Do women make as good fliers as men? Miss Amelia Earhart thinks that women are on equal flying terms with men — and certainly she has proved her theory.

We don't know. We have no theories. We have only a conviction – that the women pilots we have talked to are amazing in their skill and knowledge."

VOGUE, January 1936

*Right* America's 'First Lady of the Sky': Amelia Earhart in front of one of Steichen's photographic panels, in a room designed by Eugene Schoen in Radio City. The first woman to fly the Atlantic, she married the publisher George P. Putnam: tragically, she was to disappear over the Pacific in 1937
STEICHEN 1933

# THE DOMESTIC FRONT

'*Vogue* has always said that the
background of every woman is her home:
you can wear the loveliest clothes and
jewels, and if you wear them in a dated,
unmodish interior – well what's the good?'
VOGUE, January 1935

*Left Les Toits de
Paris*: the view
from Princess Guy
de Faucigny-
Lucinge's
'picturesque
apartment' on the
Ile de la Cité
SONIA 1929

*Right* The Hon Vita
Sackville-West, at
her Elizabethan
family house,
Knole
1927

'Since the signing of the Armistice, there has been a real renaissance of taste in all that concerns the home,' *Vogue* reported in the summer of 1919. As the havoc of the First World War began to recede into history, international society returned to its peacetime pursuits with a renewed zest. Clothes could be freely ordered from Paris once more, theatres and restaurants flourished again – and in 'all that concerns the home', from entertaining to interior decoration, there was an upsurge of creativity and interest.

*Vogue* had always enjoyed unusual access to the world of the 'makers of taste': even before the War, society figures who might normally have shied from publicity allowed themselves and their houses to be photographed for *Vogue*. During the 1920s and '30s, as interest in design and decoration grew, those whose houses appeared in the magazine ranged from peeresses and politicians to distinguished artists, musicians and writers. There were features on Charles de Beistegui's Paris apartment, designed by Le Corbusier, and Virginia Woolf's Bloomsbury drawing room, decorated by Duncan Grant and Vanessa Bell; on Theodore Roosevelt's hunting-trophy room, H. G. Wells's library, and Cole Porter's peppy music room, with its lacquered walls and zebra rugs. When the glamorous Lord and Lady Louis Mountbatten replaced their family mansion on Park Lane with an ultra-modern penthouse apartment, the results were featured in *Vogue* – and some of the most memorable photographs of the era showed beauties and hostesses such as Lady Honor Channon and Mrs William S. Paley posing amid their striking interiors in Belgravia and Beekman Place.

Interior decorating became one of the smartest of all professions. The doyenne of decorators, the American-born Elsie de Wolfe (wife of British diplomat Sir Charles Mendl) was joined in the social columns by a series of colleagues and rivals with widely-differing styles. Syrie Maugham, wife of the novelist Somerset Maugham, introduced her famous all-white interiors; Sybil Colefax and John Fowler became known for chintz and enduringly English good taste; by the mid-1930s, as decor veered between the modern and the baroque, *Vogue* was driven to conclude, 'A dominating note in decoration is less apparent in our time than with any

*Above* Lady Abdy at her dressing-table
SCHALL 1935

preceding generation.'

The tranquil grandeur of great country houses, and the way of life they represented, retained a timeless appeal for *Vogue*'s readers. Cecil Beaton regularly photographed *grandes dames* in their ancestral homes – from Mrs Vanderbilt in her magnificent library on Long Island, to the young Countess of Pembroke in the Double Cube Room at Wilton. The 'Our Lives from Day to Day' column featured endless snapshots and reports of house-parties at which guests such as Tallulah Bankhead, the Hon David Herbert and Oliver Messel played backgammon and picnicked; and writers such as Theodora Benson contributed amusing articles on the pleasures (and hazards) of country weekends.

In town apartments and country mansions alike, servants were assumed to be indispensable. ('Enlist your butler's tact over the seating-arrangements' was one blithe suggestion, in a 1938 article on giving a party.) Though *Vogue*'s cartoonists found plenty of humour in the foibles of pert parlour maids and comical chauffeurs, in general the editorial tone, where servants were concerned, was one of somewhat feudal appreciation. A popular series of articles with the general title 'My Cook Is a . . .' extolled the virtues of cooks of different nationalities ('My Cook Is a Hungarian'; 'My Cook Is an African', etc.) until skilfully and properly debunked by the novelist Lesley Blanch – a *Vogue* staff journalist – with a contribution entitled, 'My Cook Is a Catastrophe'. Only rarely was it suggested that cooking for oneself, let alone for guests, might be a pleasure.

In the nursery as in the kitchen, servants ruled. 'The entire domestic bliss of the young mother's home is balanced on the all-important corner-stone of the Nannie,' *Vogue* declared in 1929. Even the most blasé of society women were assumed to take an interest in their children, however; and there were regular features on children's clothes, suggestions for decorating the modern nursery, and photographs of well-known parents with their offspring.

Amid *Vogue*'s chronicle of society's sports, travels and amusements, reports from the domestic front had a special appeal. They kept readers informed of the latest trends and fashions in cooking, decor, entertaining – and they offered delightful, privileged glimpses into the private worlds of the rich and famous.

*Above* 'But why didn't you tell me that a terrazzo floor looked like that?'
MOURGUE 1930

*Left* A centrepiece of 'the very modern apartment' built by Le Corbusier and Pierre Jeanneret for M. Charles de Beistegui, in Paris. The 'astonishing suspended staircase', here, is of cement painted pale blue and white, with a crystal rail
BUFFOTOT 1933

*Right* Amid some controversy, Lord and Lady Louis Mountbatten's London family house (a former landmark of Park Lane) was pulled down in the 1930s, and replaced with a modern apartment block — at the top of which the Mountbattens created a stunning, two-floor penthouse apartment for themselves. The long gallery lined with Van Dycks, shown here, was designed to display part of their collection of 'pictures, jades, and plate'
MILLAR AND HARRIS 1937

# A DECORATOR OF DISTINCTION

*Opposite page:*
*top left* Lady
Mendl
BEATON 1935
*Top right* The
entrance hall of
Lady Mendl's Paris
apartment
SONIA 1929
*Bottom* The terrace
of Condé Nast's
penthouse
1930

*Below* One of
Lady Mendl's best-
known
commissions, the
penthouse of
*Vogue's*
proprietor, Condé
Nast
MATTIE EDWARDS
HEWITT 1928

"An apartment with true distinction in each of its very charming rooms is that of Lady Mendl, the decorator Elsie de Wolfe, in Paris. Throughout, old things have been used in the modern manner - a paradox that is extremely effective. The colour schemes, in particular, reflect the modern feeling, but most of the furniture and other decorations are old and very fine.

In the small salon an exceptional collection of drawings is beautifully arranged against the severely panelled walls. The sofa in this room is covered with old-gold velvet, the rug is in black and beige, and the two armchairs are covered with satin in bluish pearl-grey. Both the salon and the dining-room are panelled with old boiserie, and old fabrics in rich colourings are used for hangings and upholstery. An interesting note is the use of beige, cream, and brown throughout – outstanding colours in present-day decoration, whether it follows the modern or the old. The dining-room in Lady Mendl's apartment is panelled with blond Régence boiserie, with blond silk in the panels. There are blond silk curtains, a brown lacquer screen, a console to match the boiserie, and a brown marble mantel. The cream rug has a brown border. In Lady Mendl's bedroom, the use of cream-white, in the old, quilted, satin bed-covering and hangings and in the rug, is particularly charming."

VOGUE, September 1929

*Right* A room in Virginia Woolf's house in Tavistock Square, London. The decoration is by Duncan Grant and Vanessa Bell 1924

# A BLOOMSBURY INTERIOR

"There is at present in this country an artistic activity which is producing work more interesting and more vital than anything that has made its appearance here during the last hundred years. Moreover, many of the leading artists in this modern movement (which is derived largely from Cézanne and the French Impressionists) have turned their attention to decorative work.

Among these are Duncan Grant and Vanessa Bell, who even before the War were associated with a group of artists who produced work of this kind under the leadership of Roger Fry. The War, unfortunately, put a complete stop to this enterprise, but not before they had produced a great many charming things in the way of furniture, stuffs and pottery, practical as well as beautiful. Duncan Grant and Vanessa Bell can turn their versatile hands to anything, from the complete scheme of decoration down to the last detail of a drawing-room, to the painting of a bowl, a tile, a screen or a cushion. The picture above shows a room in the Tavistock Square house of Virginia Woolf, the brilliant author of *Jacob's Room* and *The Voyage Out*. The walls are a cool dove grey; the borders of the panels are tomato-red, while the panels themselves are a glossy white. The subjects are painted directly on to them in umbers, whites and browns, with touches of lettuce green.

Except in the painting of rooms – when with a very necessary care they supervise the workman who mixes and applies their subtle colours – Duncan Grant and Vanessa Bell carry out all their own decorative work in their studio at No 8, Fitzroy Street."

VOGUE, November 1924

*Left* The Countess
Jean de Polignac
at home
BEATON 1935

*Below right* Tea is
served
BRISSAUD 1933

*Below left* The art
of decoration
MARTY 1929

# THE MODERN APPROACH
## by Jean-Michel Frank

"Two things seem equally impossible to me: to live in a modern house where it would be a shock to walls and furniture if a Louis XV clock were put on the mantel, or to furnish a period room to such perfection that you really wonder where you will hide the telephone.

In the last few years a strong interest has sprung up for interior decoration. Care in choosing, in arranging, and taste for simplicity have become widespread. In art shows, private interiors, department stores, magazines and so on this interest is evident. It has, without doubt, become easy to decorate one's walls in a modern spirit, since mural decoration has been greatly simplified.

Why would it seem that we are faced with a relative difficulty in the choice of only modern furniture? We do admire their beautiful woods, smooth and precious, other materials, and the quality of workmanship. Perhaps the experiments in the field of modern furniture have been of two sorts: some have sought only comfort and practicality, with little regard for beauty, others have sought almost exclusively novelty and the more aesthetic side, to the neglect of comfort. It must not be forgotten that the style of decoration is determined by the type of place it is meant for. This, of course, is a principle which applies equally to clothes design."

VOGUE, April 1935

*Opposite* Mr and Mrs Harrison Williams
BEATON 1935

*Below* 'Born of a necessity, the music room in Mr and Mrs Cole Porter's Paris house centres on the piano, screened in straw marquetry, and the composer's work-table. Silver lacquer panels give the effect of mirrors, reflecting the beech-trees in the garden'
SONIA 1932

# TWO SCHOOLS OF DECOR

"When Lady Honor Channon (left) at the outset of her married life established herself as an important young hostess, she created for herself that essential background, a house, with a degree of success that many older women never attain. For her beautiful profile, and her wonderful skin and blonde colouring, her background of pastel colours and Regency decoration in Belgrave Square suits her to perfection. The now famous blue and silver dining room, inspired by a room in the Amalienburg Palace near Munich, seems to have been destined for her, and when she entertains, she has the brilliant atmosphere of an important London hostess – the atmosphere that goes with white ties, lighted chandeliers and red carpets."

VOGUE, January 1937

"The two opposing schools of decoration, the Great Baroque and the Starkly Simple, seem to have met at last. You will meet baroque carvings framing the doorways of otherwise modern rooms, and very modern plaster masks covering the lights on old panelled walls. And in much modern furniture a second glance will show its eighteenth-century inspiration. While this may not herald the beginning of a very great period of decoration, it does bring a refreshing comfort into the over-austere rooms of recent years, with their insistence upon purely functional forms. And for those who insist that our rooms express, as it has so often been put, our Restless Modern Life, perhaps this pleasant confusion is the perfect answer."

VOGUE, October 1935

*Opposite* Lady Honor Channon, wife of the diarist Henry 'Chips' Channon, in her baroque dining-room
BEATON 1937

*Below* Mrs Syrie Maugham, the influential decorator who introduced the vogue for 'all-white' rooms, in the sitting room of her London house
BEATON 1934

# AN AMERICAN STATELY HOME

"Of all the rooms in this great house, the library, dark and crowded with mementos of a lifetime, is Mrs Vanderbilt's favourite. Far more like a salon in Paris than a room one might expect to find in New York, the library tables are loaded with bibelots, with ornaments in mutton-fat jade, with vases filled with flowers, with books – some autographed, with photographs, all ceremoniously signed.

A beautiful jumble of damasks, petit-point, tapestry, and velvets, this room is thoroughly lived in. The small tables are covered with fringed velvet in the style that was so fashionable in the Paris of Proust's day before the First World War, and that is just now becoming fashionable again in this country.

The room has French Regency wood-work of oak, and Regency furniture, some pieces covered in a ripe, raspberry-red silk; others, in the French fashion, covered in the same yellow-green damask as the walls.

But the chief glory of the room is the tapestry, shown here, which was made in Brussels sometime in the seventeenth century. It represents the famous visit of Alexander the Great to Diogenes at Athens. (At that time, Alexander, master of the known world, asked the impoverished philosopher if there was anything that he could do for him. 'Yes,' said Diogenes, 'you can stand out of my light.') It is beneath this tapestry that Mrs Vanderbilt receives her intimate friends, and serves tea."

VOGUE, November 1941

# HOW TO GIVE A DINNER-PARTY
## As told by Katharine Frelinghuysen

"Good parties always excite us – even the reverberations of them. We love to know who gives them, how they are done, what makes the wheels go round. One obvious answer to the question 'Who gives them?' is 'The Americans' – whose parties possess, quite unfailingly, that mixture of vitality and perfect presentation which sparkles up the atmosphere more surely than champagne. And among Americans in general, Mrs Frederick T. Frelinghuysen in particular: so still having on the tip of our tongue those questions about how good parties are done, we decided to ask what she did.

To begin with, she says, if you want to give good parties, you must love giving them. It is one of the greatest fallacies to believe that a party 'makes itself'; that it 'either goes, or it doesn't'. Behind every kind of success lies hard work.

Mrs Frelinghuysen believes that, at her parties, her greatest asset is her cook. Both she *and* the cook give the party, and her entire household is made to feel that the success of the occasion lies in their hands. Then, there is the manner in which you select your guests. Don't cling to the same faces, who will inevitably contribute the same type of conversation. Shuffle in the spice of something new. Ask people who bring with them a quality of gaiety and the tang of a new personality. If you give a party *for* some one person, select from your list those whom you feel your guest of honour will most wish to see, and most keenly enjoy, irrespective of the fact that these people may have dined with you the week before.

Every party menu should be planned in advance with one's cook, down to the smallest detail, then written out and hung in the kitchen. On the day before the party, a copy with all details of service is pinned in the pantry. When she is dressing for a party, Mrs Frelinghuysen always calls down on the house phone to give last-minute directions and a reminder that the champagne be iced to exactly the right degree. She makes a definite point of a last-minute glance at her table, something no good hostess will ever neglect.

Cocktails and canapés can start any party off very right or very wrong, so have a care in the choice and calibre. There should always be a choice of two cocktails, such as Martinis and Old-Fashioneds, with sherry at hand. And if you remember some guest's special cocktail idiosyncrasy, you will be blessed eternally. One hot hors-d'oeuvre should always be planned, and it should be really hot, handed round in a silver hot-water dish and continually renewed. Better to keep guests waiting a little if necessary for fresh canapés from the kitchen than offer those unimaginative bits of paste-on-toast, those dreary, forlorn affairs over which the late-comer must pretend interest. The simplest canapés, provided they are crisp and hot, are the most popular. Also, in the drinking category, be sure that the butler is instructed to offer a whisky-and-soda to any guest who may refuse champagne, because, now and then people hesitate to ask for it, and there's nothing more pleasant than the feeling of individual consideration.

The menu itself should always have an air of excitement – a little frivolity must creep in, either in the food or in the way the food is served. Above all, the table arrangements must have imagination and charm.

VOGUE, September 1936

*Opposite* The setting for a perfect party: Mrs Frederick T. Frelinghuysen's brown and white dining room, with its twin tables of polished wood, mirrored bamboo screens and unusual combination of pewter and silver
L NYHOM 1936

*Below* The perfect hostess: Mrs Frelinghuysen, in a gingham dress by Mainbocher
1932

CHOSEN SURROUNDINGS
*Right* Mrs William S. Paley, in the drawing room of her Beekman Place house, 'which she herself decorated as a charming expression of her own taste, her own varied interests.' Mr and Mrs Paley's collection of modern paintings was 'fundamental to the decoration' HORST 1937

*Left* Coco Chanel, arbiter of elegance, in her private apartment at the Ritz in Paris BERARD 1937

# THE AMERICAN WEEKEND VISIT

"The week-end visit has become a very great favourite in this country as it has in England. On Long Island, a great many people keep their houses open all the year round, and even in the winter, though they spend the middle of the week in town, they pass the week-ends in the country.

. . . If week-end guests arrive at tea time, then while they are partaking of tea, a maid or valet unpacks the luggage and, when the guests go to their rooms to dress for dinner, is there to draw the bath and generally to assist with the dressing, unless the guest has brought his or her personal servant. At the large house-parties, dinner demands full evening dress, though in an intimate circle, one often sees the men in dinner jackets, and the women in the charming trailing tea-gowns of the moment.

Every one should be present and on time, which does not mean on the stroke of the appointed hour, but at least five minutes earlier. The party assembles in the drawing-room before going in to dinner, which is served from eight to half-past eight in the larger country houses and thus allows plenty of time for the sports that add so much joy to a visit in the country.

Even at a large house-party it is not customary to have place-cards on the dinner-table – though they may be used at the first dinner – and the women usually seat themselves in every other chair so that the men may take the alternating vacant places. This plan of seating results in a much happier combination than could be planned by the most clever hostesses. Luncheon is a more informal affair, and breakfast is the most elastic of meals. At breakfast time, the table is set in the dining-room for the men, while trays are usually taken to the rooms of the women.

The guest room in the really smart house is thoroughly well-equipped

*Above* Upon one's arrival at a house-party, attractive maid and obsequious valet are at the door to render the first services of hospitality impartially to guest and guest's dog'
JOHN BARBOUR 1920

without being overfurnished or overdecorated. A common habit of unnecessary thoughtfulness is to cover the dressing-table with many superfluous toilet articles. This is a mistake, for all guests come prepared with such accessories, and if any are forgotten the maid will quickly supply the guest with what has been omitted. On the other hand, the crowded table leaves no room for the guest's possessions, and there is also the inconvenient possibility of packing some articles belonging to the house, in the hurry of departure. A writing-table completely fitted with stationery, telegraph blanks, and time-tables, and a clock set with the time of the household, are almost essential for the guest's convenience.

Notwithstanding the fact that there is a delusion that tipping is not the custom in this country, it is just as well for the hostess to seem unconscious of the fact that the guest who wishes to make a success in the servants' hall and be well looked after on future visits, tips rather lavishly. If the guest is a man, he tips the butler, the footman who valets him, and the chauffeur, while a woman with her husband remembers only the maids with whom she comes in contact. A woman alone tips the butler, the maids, and the chauffeur as well.

The hostess is not expected to appear at an early hour to speed the parting guest, therefore it is tactful to say good-bye on retiring and to express more fully one's enjoyment in the 'bread and butter' letter, which follows within a few days of the visit."

VOGUE, 1920

'If the guest is unfortunate enough to arrive at that awkward hour when the hostess is dressing for dinner, competent servants make up for her absence by numerous other discreet attentions'
JOHN BARBOUR 1920

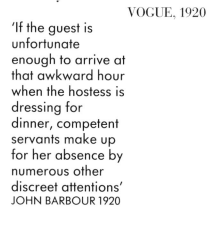

*Left* Blenheim Palace, near Oxford, built by a grateful nation for the 1st Duke of Marlborough in the eighteenth century. Members of the 10th Duke's family are seen here at the towering North Entrance
BEATON 1938

*Right* In a scene reminiscent of an eighteenth-century Gainsborough painting, Sir John Dashwood returns from shooting to greet his family in the colonnade at West Wycombe Park, their country house
BEATON 1932

# THE GREAT ENGLISH HOUSE

"To know and understand England at all, you must know the life of the English country house, for English gentle folk live in the country, not in town, and these country houses are their homes. However big and comfortable their town houses may be, they don't really count. These people come up to town for the season, for a week or two, or for all winter, perhaps, from Tuesday to Friday, and then they go home, to Hampshire or Kent or Sussex, where they belong. There they keep all the treasures that the family has been accumulating for generations, the galleries full of pictures, the libraries full of books, the cabinets full of old china and glass, the family silver, the family ghosts and skeletons, which give to the house its character and that human friendliness and that glamour which only come with age.

So the most important thing about the week-end party in the country in England is the house itself. You hear people say, 'We are spending Whitsun or Easter at such and such a house,' much more often than you hear them say, 'We are going to stay with so and so.' Indeed, to hear people talk, you would sometimes think that men and women only existed as more or less insignificant appendages to the country places they happen to own. They are more owned and run by their houses than the other way round."

VOGUE, May 1927

*Right* 'Mr Evelyn Waugh, the novelist, was snapped at a house-party at Madresfield Court with the youngest daughter of the house, Lady Dorothy Lygon.' 1932

*Below* A country idyll: 'the lady studying a large portfolio is Mrs Reed Vreeland, noted as a hostess and a person of unusual charm, and the placid beauty sewing so peacefully is Mrs Sacheverell Sitwell'.
BEATON 1933

# FRIDAY TO MONDAY
## by Theodora Benson

"I love a house party where there is nothing particular to do but walk and talk and read. But if people don't want to do nothing, the host does better by providing them with an occupation they don't like rather than none. If they are forced to play charades and hate them, they can take each other aside and have a cosy time confiding how foul they think it. Even a dreadful party where everyone quarrels provides a lot of conversation. I love a sightseeing party, though sightseeing, I admit, should be very optional. The worst house-party of all is the very organised one where you are whisked around to lunch with the neighbours. But even so, the host is justified in standing unshakeably upon

these two slogans; 'Dash it all, who's house is it, anyway?' and 'Well, after all, they needn't come again!'

The chief obligation of the guest is to be adaptable. Indeed, he should be imperturbable. No matter what happens the guest must not embarrass the host.

As a guest, the first thing I look for in my bedroom is a vase of flowers, the second a wastepaper basket and the third bedside biscuits. (That is excluding the seasonal question of a fire.) I consider it annoying, but not alienating, if there isn't a well-stocked desk, also hangers. If I forget a hot water bottle in hot water bottle weather, it is kindness not duty if they supply one.

Certainly it is daunting if the house is too cold; it coops the party up in a bunch, as they have to huddle together over the fire. Some sort of exercise or activity ought to be available, as the thing about men is that very often they are in the city and work hard from morning to night, so that they want their exercise provided for them at the week-end, but cannot possibly take an ordinary walk. It is annoying of them to be unable to take walks, but even so the host should not feel apologetic if he has no tennis, golf or shooting. One or another is useful. Still, if the guest has the chance of hacking with the host, of driving the sheep or cutting the kail, and does not want to, it then becomes up to the guest to find his own amusement. Let him go and pick beechnuts by himself, or what not.

The intellectual party, where you play children's games, may come anywhere in comfort from one of these extremes to the other. It is a very variable and toss-up party. The games sound dismal and daunting, particularly paper ones, but are often fun.

I remember a week-end when I and another girl were joint hostesses. I shall never forget the fantastic spate of telegrams that came for us. Every single person, on account of 'flu or some equally watertight reason, failed – except Lord Donegall. And by the time we had the bright idea of putting him off, he had left already for the station. We didn't know him very well – you know, we just called him 'You' – he had never been to stay before, and it is a reasonable bet he never will again.

But none of us minded terribly. Lord Donegall was very agreeable and very amusing. I imagine that some day there will appear in his reminiscences – 'Talking of dull week-ends, the dullest I ever spent was at the invitation of Theodora Benson.' But I don't remember it as a searing mortification, and after all that was about the worst fiasco that can happen at a week-end."

VOGUE, January 1936

*Below* The Hon David Herbert and Miss Tallulah Bankhead 1934

*Left* Mrs Reginald
C. Vanderbilt and
her daughter,
Gloria
EDWARD F. FOLEY
1928

*Right* At tea-time
BENITO 1941

avec
excus
a ma
Bris...
et J...
BE
NI
TO

*Right* The song-writer Irving Berlin with his wife and their daughters Mary Ellin and Linda Louise, photographed in their New York apartment
STEICHEN 1932

Nursery World – the fashionable child: *clockwise from top left* Lepape 1918; Marty 1925; Harriet Meserole 1924; Lepape 1921

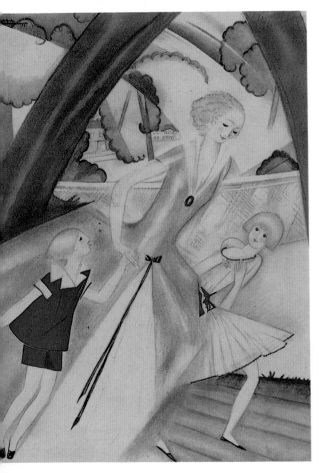

# NURSERY WORLD – TRADITIONAL

"Nannie holds the door open, gravely to announce 'The Lady Caroline Blackwood' . . . and then adds in a most persuasive undertone, 'Say how-do-you-do to the lady, darling.' Rocking ever so slightly on her toes, regarding the caller intently, Lady Caroline extends a friendly little hand before turning again to the absorbing business of walking.

Let those who think our world tottering ask themselves just this: 'Stands nursery tea (complete with nannie, old-style) where it did?' It does. Nurseries have not yet gone all synthetic, and our quaint new world is neither quaint nor brave enough yet to dispense with the tall fender, the white apron and – the lap! The English nannie is still (with the English butler) one of our most sought-after visible exports.

As Nurse Bartholomew busies herself with bath preparations and supper is put to warm on the nursery heating apparatus, Lady Caroline hospitably shares a game of ball with the visitor. The small daughter of the Marchioness of Dufferin likes 'company', and already shows definite signs of an unshakeable 'poise' that will probably make her one of the *grandes dames* of the 1960s."

VOGUE, April 1933

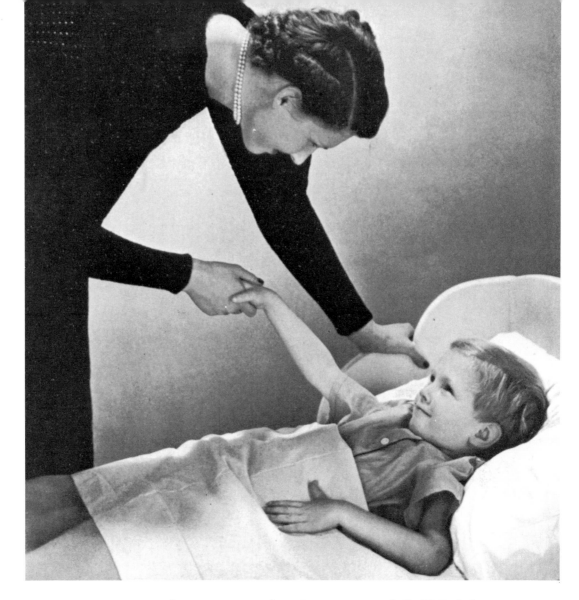

*Left* 'Once upon a time children were looked on as responsibilities; now they are esteemed as entertainers. The Victorian mother wept over her children, and placed her cool hand on their fevered brow. The present-day mother screams with laughter at her children, and does not apply her hand to their brow, nor to the other end of their anatomy, which probably accounts for a good deal'
FISH 1923

*Right* Should you kiss your child good-night – or should you shake hands with him?
STEICHEN

*Left* Lady Caroline Blackwood, daughter of the Marquess and Marchioness of Dufferin and Ava, with her nanny. *Vogue* predicted that she would be 'one of the *grandes dames* of the 1960s'. In fact, Lady Caroline became a well-known writer and was to marry the artist Lucian Freud, the musician Israel Citkovitz, and the poet Robert Lowell
JOHN HAVINDEN 1933

# NURSERY WORLD – MODERN
## by Gretta Palmer

"Paternity is more than a cult – it is a vocation among some of the people who set the pace. Their enthusiasm may take one of several forms ... They confer with the principal of the progressive school, call on the psychoanalyst at the drop of a rattle, and are changing parenthood into a learned profession.

These are some of the questions the Progressive Papas have under debate:

Does it encourage Oedipus complexes to let children kiss their mothers good-night? Or should they only shake hands? Should a child be taught to say his prayers? Should fourteen-year-old radicals join picket-lines? Is it best to change nurses every three months, so that the infant will not get a fixation that might disturb his hypothetical married life? Should a child call his parents by their first names? Will lead soldiers make a child combative? Should children be given nursery-size Martinis so that they will not take alcohol too seriously? Does every youngster pass through a stage as a biter? If Father gets tight, should this phenomenon be explained to the child? Will psychoanalysis cure nightmares? Should children be encouraged to wander into the room where Mother or Daddy is taking a bath?

Whatever this generation turns out, they cannot complain that they did not enjoy the best thought of the most professional-sounding fathers of all time.

VOGUE, January 1937

# LADIES' LADIES
## by Cecil Beaton

"The pages of fashion magazines bloom with the beauties of the day, enhanced by jewels from Cartier, décor by Tchelitchew, flowers from Max Schling. But invariably the most important person, perhaps, in the life of the professional or society beauty, the lady's maid, goes unheralded and unsung.

Few people realize how great a part a maid plays in the life of her lady. Yet the maid may see even more of her mistress than the husband does. (This is why jealous husbands often instinctively resent their wives' maids.) From the moment the mistress is awake, and often as not until she goes to sleep, she is entirely dependent on Miss Smith, who knows her every foible, who knows exactly how she will react under every circumstance, and who is trusted quite automatically for her devotion and discretion . . . To-day, in their world in New York, London and Paris, certain of these ladies' maids are themselves well-known personalities, and could no

doubt supply much intriguing information. From what ladies' maids would you like to hear? Would you like to be told that Mrs Harrison Williams sleeps between a fresh pair of sheets each night? But alas, Mrs Williams' maid, Helen, has always avoided the limelight. She shuns publicity, and balks at every attempt to make her answer. We have heard it whispered that she is a forceful Briton, extremely strict in every respect, and if, for instance, she doesn't like a particular evening dress, then that particular evening dress is never given a chance. Are you interested in the fact that Mrs Harold E. Talbott's Agnes Dawson has had to become an authority on clothes for sporting life? That she knows the correct outfit for everything from hunting to golfing?

Miss Nellie Watkins, who lives at Lismore Castle, Ireland, and at Carlton Gardens, London, with Lady Charles Cavendish, says that her mistress is a very normal and good-natured person with a few strange idiosyncrasies. Miss Nelles tells us that her mistress never wears a darned stocking, no matter how small the mend; that she gets the worst case of train fever she has ever seen; and that the jitters begin an hour before it is time to start; that she wears three different négligées while dressing, treating the performance as a three-act play.

The typical maid of to-day must be ready to face all emergencies. On the telephone, she is informed that to-morrow her mistress is leaving for Paris, London, New York, Peking, Timbuctoo, Madagascar. 'Pack at once. There is some last-minute shopping for you to do. Send telegrams putting off my dinner. Get tickets, see to the trunks.' To the maid are left all sorts of decisions. She has to judge the amount of space to be allowed in the trunks, what to declare at the customs. She must be able to speak foreign languages and also be chaperon and secretary. Very likely, she is asked to shake a cocktail, and, if she is perfection itself, she should also be a beauty expert and a trained seamstress. She lays out the stockings ready to be slipped on with the toes tucked inward. She can prolong the life of a dress with frequent steamings and careful pressings. And she knows exactly when the cleaning of a dress is beyond her and when it must be sent out.

Her position is of extreme importance. She is important to her mistress, and, down-stairs in the servants' dining-hall, she is honoured as such and considered the ambassadress of her betters. In large households, where formality is kept as rigidly below-stairs as up, she answers to her mistress' name, so that when Mrs Williams is at Blenheim for the week-end, Helen, below-stairs, becomes Mrs Williams. But the Duchess of Devonshire's maid takes precedence over Helen, in the servants' hall, and is taken into dinner by

*Above* The perfect 'Lady's lady': Mrs Harold E. Talbott's maid, Agnes Dawson
BEATON 1935

*Left* 'Hannah downs tools on Mrs Dinwiddie when the table is set for a large dinner-party and all the employment agencies are closed'
FISH 1928

the valet of the Duke of Marlborough. The butler is host, and the housekeeper is hostess. The visiting guests' maids correspond in rank to their respective mistresses, and, if there is more than one duchess at the party, the maid of the ranking duchess sits at the butler's right."

VOGUE, August 1935

# WAR: THE NEW SPIRIT

'From a purely social viewpoint there's a lot to be said for the new spirit . . . It clears the air as if by magic of much that is sham, silly and pretentious'

VOGUE, November 1939

*Above* Mrs William Wesson Jervey head of Washington's AWVF canteens
ERIC 1942

*Opposite* 'Mrs Robert Lewis Fisher, volunteer in America's Office of Civilian Defense, nails up a curtain for a practice blackout.'
BALKIN 1942

151

*Above* 'Mrs Max
Aitken surveys an
aluminium
mountain conjured
up by the
eloquence of her
father-in-law, Lord
Beaverbrook, to
be poured into our
precious planes'
1940

In the spring of 1939, as the prospect of war in Europe loomed once again, *Vogue* sought to reassure its readers that the forthcoming social season would be as brilliant as ever. 'There'll be pomp and pageantry in plenty for debutantes this summer', a May issue announced confidently. 'The stage is set . . . and the skies must fall indeed before we'll ring down the curtain one second sooner than is necessary.' Such defiant optimism proved short-lived, however. 'This season was different,' British *Vogue* reflected soberly in July; and by the time the autumn issues appeared on the bookstalls, the skies had fallen indeed. Britain and France were at war with Germany; before long the United States would be in action also; and the old, heedless life of international society vanished from sight, like Cinderella on the stroke of midnight.

In all three national editions of *Vogue*, frivolity was replaced by a new mood of staunch, yet thoughtful, dedication to the war-effort. 'Septembre 1939 . . . Adieu la Mode!' wrote French *Vogue* wistfully. An editorial in the British edition observed, 'Our hearts are back in the right place,' adding robustly, 'There's a lot to be said for the new spirit.' American *Vogue*, addressing a readership still at peace, declared, 'American women are turning their eyes forward, turning their hands to directing airplane controls, gathering relief funds, campaigning for domestic issues . . . hands no less helpful for being well-gloved.' After the Occupation of Paris in June 1940, French *Vogue* suspended publication, rather than co-operate with the enemy; but British *Vogue* (though reduced to a flimsy monthly) soldiered on, providing news from Europe when possible, and continually exchanging reports, articles and photographs with the American parent-edition. 'Bringing out a luxury magazine in a Blitzkreig is rather like dressing for dinner in the jungle,' British *Vogue* wrote wryly, after the London office was bombed; the American edition, reviewing *Vogue*'s role in 'a world embattled and bleeding', summed up, 'A grave situation isn't helped by glum faces or defeatism.' Keeping up appearances – always *Vogue*'s, forte – was now a matter of national morale, rather than personal pride.

In Paris, before the Occupation, there was an illusory air of 'business as usual'; but the nightclubs, filled with Allied officers on leave, closed early, and the word 'Abri' – air-raid shelter – loomed over the tables at the Ritz. The exquisite Mrs Reginald (Daisy) Fellowes knitted ostentatiously throughout the curtailed spring Collections; and celebrated hostesses such as Lady Mendl and the Duchess of Windsor replaced lavish party-giving with war-charity work. In London, well-known leaders of fashion appeared in unfamiliar new guises – supervising canteens, driving allied generals, nursing with the VADs, or serving in the women's Forces. As one of American *Vogue*'s regular reports from Britain put it, 'Everyone has a new set of values now.'

Throughout 1940 and '41, American *Vogue* skilfully balanced its editorial content to reflect both the realities of war abroad and the requirements of peace at home. Features on fashion, beauty, parties and holidays were interspersed now with reports on London bomb-damage, American volunteers with the RAF Eagle Squadron and the plight of refugees in Europe. Readers were urged to contribute to 'Aid for Britain' campaigns; and American women, both at home and abroad, were shown running war-relief charities, raising funds for the Allies, and spear-heading America's own civilian defence preparations. When, in December 1941, the attack on Pearl Harbor brought the United States into the Second World War, Tom Treanor, writing in American *Vogue*, recorded, 'The social decks were cleared for action . . . women in slacks began appearing in overwhelming numbers at Red Cross classes, signal corps, rifle corps, air-raid details.' He concluded, 'We are taking a lot of things in our stride now . . .' Cecil Beaton had become a war-correspondent with the British Ministry of Information, photographing bomb-damage and front-line troops. The glamorous playwright Clare Boothe Luce was now a respected war reporter. Lee Miller, formerly the most beautiful of *Vogue* models, donned a tin helmet and followed the Allies into France, recording the horrors of war for a *Vogue* readership which, until five years before, had thrived on accounts of costume-balls and country house-parties.

Society and *Vogue* alike had suffered a sea-change. 'There's a lot to be said for the new spirit,' British *Vogue* had observed in September 1939; after the Second World War, the old spirit was banished for ever.

*Below* At the New York City Defense Recreation Center 1942

# PARIS NOW

"Paris in the fourth month of the war is an attractive, comfortable, almost normal city with an intimate, quasi-country charm. Although you can now enjoy such luxuries as smart hats and plentiful taxis, nobody will look at you askance if you go hatless or ride your bicycle.

There is an allied flavour to the uniforms in Paris, with English Army, Navy, and Air Force officers passing through; and with lots of Polish aviators in bluish-grey waiting to be sent to join English squadrons. Young RAF flyers

on their first Paris leaves sit in every *boîte* where there is music, tapping out rhythms to the tantalizing music. These boys are refreshing, but heart-breaking – with their infantile faces.

Bill Taylor, one of New York's popular bachelors, recently stopped in Paris with two young British naval aviators in tow. Bill volunteered in the British naval aviation and was given a commission immediately on his American naval flying experience. The three officers created a stir in Paris with their elegant white caps, their silver-topped canes,

and their British insistence that they change for dinner in a Paris that hasn't seen a shirt-front since the war began.

Paris is beginning to open up a little at night, to take care of the 'leave' exuberance. However, nightclubs throw you out bodily at eleven, leaving you nowhere to go except to some private house. The theatres are opening, and nearly every opening is a benefit performance. Noel Coward arranged a benefit performance of *Spring Fever* which continues to play to full houses. The Elsa Maxwell movie, *Women's Hotel,* brought in huge war benefit receipts.

Scheherazade is open from six until eleven. It is gay, and the music is good. Other places where you can hear music are the Boeuf Sur le Toit and the Elysées Bar, where the sensational 'Môme' Piaf sings. She is the new war songstress. You can hardly get standing-room at the Elysées, and her records are collectors' items.

The moment the military element turned up in Paris, women began wishing they had ordered less practical clothes. The men clamour for attractive, almost frivolous clothes and dinner-dresses at night. . . ."

VOGUE, January 1940

*Above* Business as usual: earning much-needed export dollars, a model from Schiaparelli's wartime collection
ERIC 1940

*Opposite* 'Artist's Abri'. *Vogue's* illustrator Carl Erickson ('Eric') and his family, in their air-raid shelter, a converted cellar in their house at Senlis, outside Paris
ERIC 1940

# PARIS SIDELIGHTS

"Paris gradually grows more normal . . . When you go to be fitted at Moly-neux he complains that he has so many fittings he will never get through the day. You can hardly believe that a few weeks ago he feared he might never make another jacket. His midseason opening was like a theatrical première: actresses, smart Parisians, Madame la Générale Gamelin, Noel Coward, reporters, resident buyers. Mrs Reginald Fellowes knitted throughout the collection. Captain Molyneux sat in his usual corner. There were four mannequins instead of fifteen, thirty models instead of a hundred – but those thirty clearly struck the informal note of the moment.

The Ritz is still the smartest, most crowded meeting place. The Vendôme dining-room overflows at lunch, the Cambon bar seethes at all times – it is now full of Royal Air Force men.

Mrs Reginald Fellowes and her family, Madame Schiaparelli and her daughter Gogo, Lady Mendl, the Comtesse de Montgomery and Mrs Corrigan all live on the Ritz first floor. Dropping in for a drink means visiting from one room to the next, perhaps meeting the Sacha Guitrys, Mlle Chanel, Jean Cocteau, who also have rooms there.

In other parts of Paris, friends living in the same quarter arrange to call on one another regularly. Friends from farther off stay the night – a throwback to carriage days. Mr Bullitt, the American Ambassador, has given several informal, much-appreciated parties. The Lopez-Willshaws have buffet suppers every Wednesday and people put their names down for invitations not later than Monday, since the crowd gets bigger every week.

Lady Mendl's Sunday lunch parties at Versailles set the key for casual entertaining. Small tables are covered with multi-coloured oil cloth; on the big buffet is one hot dish, usually corn beef hash, which everyone adores, and vegetable and fruit salads. Guests take away the dishes, sweep up crumbs and play Chinese checkers and backgammon – their winnings go to the Bal Tabarin Soup Kitchen for Actors.

Conversation more often turns from the war to who is wearing what – nothing will persuade Frenchwomen to wear uniform except on duty. Mrs Reginald Fellowes wore two enamel clips at the points of her tailored collar, like military ensignias. She still wears her hair brushed up (so does Madame Schiaparelli and Madame Lopez-Willshaw) with a ribbon bow tying the puff on top. Suzy's most popular dinner hat is a red velvet skull cap with a puff of velvet on top and a heavy black mesh veil. The Duchess of Windsor and Mrs Fellowes wear the puff and veil without the skull cap.

English officers' polished boots are influencing French shoes. Some women wear dark spats, or high rubber boots, for the Parisian with war work to do rises early and walks to the nearest metro."

VOGUE, January 1940

# OUR LIVES IN WARTIME LONDON

*Above* Actors and audience dance in the aisles at the Hippodrome
FELIKS TOPOLSKI 1940

*Opposite* 'The way things are at the Dorchester'. On the roof of the Dorchester in Park Lane, air-raid spotters stand sentinel; below them, guests dance to Lew Stone's band. 'Some dress – some don't; some wear hats – some don't'
BEATON 1941

"From a purely social viewpoint there's a lot to be said for the new spirit. There is, for instance, the fact that it clears the air as if by magic of much that is sham, silly and pretentious; kills chi-chi deader than a doornail, finds better work for idle tongues than mere idle gossip. Go, these days, to any of the erstwhile playtime haunts of London, those west-end cocktail bars and hotel lounges that buzzed with malice every morning before lunch and every evening before dinner. Compared with what they used to be a month or two ago you'll find an atmosphere different as chalk from cheese and bracing as a gust of wind in foggy places. The 'buzz' remains – but it comes from conversation which is purposeful instead of pointless. Because of National Service, you'll see few with more than just the odd half-hour to spare before going on to various (often whole-time) jobs. You may see Lady Castlereagh, for instance, dashing in between lectures in her daily course of training as a VAD – neat as a pin in navy tailor-made and scarlet skirt (tailor-mades, in slickest form, seem the generally accepted wartime 'civvie' wear); Lady O'Neill sitting in a 'huddle' with her sister, Lady Long, the latter being questioned on her work as nurse in a country hospital – both of them, meanwhile, wearing identical suits of dark green jersey cloth; Mrs Newall, hatless, wrapped in the bright green linen tunic of the WVS; Lady Beatty, en route for the country and work of an organising kind.

You may hear news of those too occupied to get away to London, like the Duchess of Marlborough, working hard down at Blenheim with her unit of WATS. (Blenheim Palace has recently become the wartime home of Malvern College) and the Duchess of Sutherland, who has only just returned from Alaska, and is now busy up in her own particular part of Scotland.

In the evenings, life holds many compensations for the dismalness of blackouts. Such as cosy, unplanned 'get-together' parties in someone's house, with buffet meals. Sometimes someone will leave early, to work in an all-night canteen, as does Mrs Peter Thursby; to report for duty as ambulance driver, like Lady Betty Baldwin, or as a member of the Women's Auxiliary Fire Service, like Mrs Ronald Aird. And over and above the atmosphere of war rises the warmth, the pleasant content created by people temporarily relaxed and at ease, glad of a lit room and glowing fire, glad there is no question of having to go in search of entertainment."

VOGUE, November 1939

HANDS ACROSS
THE SEA
*Opposite*
'Distinguished
Visitors to
America'.
Promoting Anglo-
American
relations, in the
early stages of the
war, was a priority
for the British
government:
Alfred Duff
Cooper, seen here
with his celebrated
wife Lady Diana,
embarked on a
lecture-tour,
'speaking on
world politics'
around North
America.
'Completely
untemperamental,
never missing a
train, the Coopers
leap happily from
Maine to Canada
to California,
having a movie-
star success',
wrote *Vogue*
HORST 1940

*Right* 'More Aid to
Britain'. Mrs Seton
Lindsay checks a
shipment of
surgical dressings
for the American
Hospital in Britain.
'Bannered behind
her, one of the Aid
to Britain emblems
sold everywhere,
worn by everyone'
ERIC 1941

*Right* At Dudley House, sorting house for all the gifts America sent to Britain via the Red Cross; 'Lady Ward, watches Lady Alistair Innes-Ker and a fellow-helper dragging in a sack of donated clothing'
BEATON 1941

*Opposite, top left* The Red Cross Motor Corps. Mrs Rand Smith and Mrs John H. Phipps transporting Roll Call supplies 1941

*Opposite, top right* Mrs Frederick T. Frelinghuysen (*far left*) serves food at the Soldiers' and Sailors' Club on old Murray Hill.
TONI FRISSELL 1942

*Opposite, bottom right* Mrs Vincent Astor (*far left*) planning the Navy Relief Benefit with (*left to right*) her sister, Mrs Cushing Roosevelt; Mrs Lawrence Lowman; Lieutenant-Commander Walter Winchell, USNR; Lieutenant-Commander John T. Tuthill, USNR; and, seated, Ensign Nathaniel Benchley, USNR
TONI FRISSELL 1942

# HELPING HANDS, BRITISH AND AMERICAN

"At the American's Women's Club, which now houses the bombed Dudley House organisation, a strong blast of camphor and moth balls wafts across the impressive threshold. Bales of clothing, new and old; raw wool, blankets, layettes complete even to safety pins and talcum; husky lumber jackets, fur coats, stockings, flannel nightgowns, boots, shoes. . . . This is the sorting house for all the gifts which America sends us via the Red Cross. *Bundles for Britain, British War Relief* . . . all the many organisations are dealt with here. Lady Ward, American-born, heads the organisation which, begun in her own home, Dudley House, continues its magnificent work at the American Women's Club in Grosvenor Street."
VOGUE, March 1941

"Suddenly women in America are absorbed in learning, thoroughly, ways to help their country. As volunteers, they are learning to fold parachutes, to dissect car motors; they are studying ground courses in flying, plotting map routes, and memorizing telegraph codes. They are learning to keep hospital charts, and to feed quickly masses of troops on the move. If war does come, they will be ready to do Government service, or to take over jobs released by men on combat duty."
VOGUE, February 1941

"Mrs Frederick Frelinghuysen spends much of her time at the Soldiers' and Sailors' Club, where the men find food, fun and shelter. At a recent Sunday afternoon open house, 600 men milled through the rooms, ate turkey, spaghetti, and cakes. Later they watched the entertainment planned by Mrs Frelinghuysen, chairman of the Entertainment Committee.

The Club has sleeping accommodation at 50 cents a night, a canteen open every day, dancing classes and Thursday and Saturday night parties. Casual, pleasant, the club on old Murray Hill has a sign over the buffet: 'Chew your food, say your prayers and save your pennies'."

VOGUE, March 1942

"Mrs Vincent Astor spends her days working for the families of the Navy men. Mrs Astor's daily rounds include selling tickets, making speeches and persuading stars to do their acts at the Navy Relief Benefit scheduled for Madison Square Garden on March 10, from which the committees hope to clear $100,000. As Chairman of the Women's Division, Mrs Astor's job now is to make the Benefit a success."

VOGUE, March 1942

*Opposite* 'Mrs Syrie Maugham has had the bright idea of launching a New York shop, "The Market of the Americas", and devoting the proceeds to the Allied cause. She is selling Mexican flowers to girls whose outfits bloom as brilliantly' WILLAUMEZ 1943

# ADAPTABLE ROOMS
## by Syrie Maugham

"In our new way of life, everything must be as easy and labour-saving, as well as space- and money-saving, as possible. Our eating arrangements should be casual and apparently without effort. Our rooms will combine living, eating, and sleeping – so must our furniture adapt itself to many uses, and be carefully chosen with this in view.

I propose to offer a few suggestions on the essentials, for, of course, there is no end to the possibilities that occur to one. Beds that can be used as sofas; banquettes that turn into beds or dining-room seats; collapsible chairs – slip-covered – that seat the extra guests and yet fold up and go into a cupboard; and the various forms of dining and occasional tables. Remember that double-duty rooms can never achieve an untrammelled, serene look – but one can feature the clutter, use it to cosy up the place. (Have your sewing, the magazines, the unanswered letters all within reach – but keep them segregated each in its separate basket.)

Buying fresh flowers is now a strain on many budgets, so make your rooms so gay that they flower themselves. Don't hesitate about repeating the same colour accent in a neutral-coloured room . . . frankly harp on it. Or go to the other extreme and mix all colours boldly.

I am not suggesting building things in, as it is almost impossible to get this done. But a recessed bed, set between a pair of wardrobes or a pair of bookcases, gives much the same effect and is space-saving, practical and elegant (see the sketch above left). A divan bed is the easiest way of providing extra lounging and sleeping space: all that is required is a pretty covered mattress, a box-spring set on legs, and sufficient cushions to make it comfortable. A mirror on the wall facing the windows, and brilliant curtains hung high and looped back, give an effect of lightness in a dark room.

Screens covered with unrationed American cloth and decorated with coloured tape (say magenta tape criss-crossed on a green screen) make a place to stick invitations, photographs, and so on. I have covered an ugly door very effectively in this way, and found it added to the gaiety of the room.

Some rooms lend themselves to a long table set between the windows, jutting into the room, with chairs on either side – as in the illustration on the left. Open-fronted hanging shelves house the table china or pottery, chosen with decoration as well as usefulness in view. Or a flap table with one flap down when not in use may be preferred. On it set a lamp and a few papers that can easily be pushed aside at meal times. In smaller rooms, the ever-useful card-tables, with waterproof loose covers over their green baize tops, serve as dining tables.

The banquette, that irresistible piece of furniture, takes many forms. It can do duty as a bed, as well as a sofa and dining seats. Folding mattresses, such as are used to lie on in summer gardens, set on edge against the wall, form comfortable backs. Drawers built along the base of the banquette give ample space and serve the purpose of a chest of drawers. A pair of old sofas with one end of each cut off and set at right angles, forms a very satisfactory banquette, but of course does not do double duty as bed and sofa."

VOGUE, October 1943

# THE NEW COOKING

"Throughout England cooking is topic A in conversation. Having learnt to cook lately is no handicap – you don't miss the dollop of butter, pint of cream and half a dozen eggs that pre-war cooks flung in haphazardly. Harrods' grocery department hold a cooking demonstration each afternoon from 3-4, where you can pick up hundreds of hints on making the most of your food.

The following recipes are deliciously simple, foolproof to amateurs and interesting to professionals.

### Potato Entrée

Take 2 lbs potatoes, 1 lb sausages, 1 small cabbage. Boil potatoes and cabbage, mash with salt, pepper and a little nutmeg. Grease a dish; place a layer of potatoes, one of sausage meat, with potatoes on top. Sprinkle with breadcrumbs and grated cheese, dot with margarine. Bake for ¾ hour.

### Rice à la Kischenef

Take 5 ozs rice, 2 apples, 1 teaspoonful ground cinnamon, 1 tablespoonful jam or a handful of currants and sultanas, 1 tablespoonful sugar, vanilla for flavouring. Cook the rice in milk and water (or household milk powder) until it is creamy. Peel apples, dice and mix with rice. Add sugar, cinnamon, dried fruit or jam, vanilla. Mix well, put in a soufflé dish and bake for 25 minutes.

### Savoury Prunes

Stew one prune per person in a little water. Put on a sieve to drain, but keep hot. Fry a rasher of streaky bacon per person. Toast a square of bread for each person and fry in bacon fat. Roll a rasher round each prune and place on fried bread. (Toasting bread before frying takes less fat and makes it crisper and more savoury.)

### Russian Borsch

Take 2 beetroots, 2 carrots, ½ small cabbage, 2 potatoes, ½ tablespoonful vinegar, 1 dessertspoonful sugar, ½ teaspoonful salt. Clean vegetables and chop up small. Boil for an hour in 8 soupcupfuls of water, with salt. Add sugar and vinegar, and let boil for a few minutes longer. For the Polish variety, use only beetroots, thinly sliced; cook as above, but end by stirring slowly into the soup a paste made from a dessertspoonful of flour and a little cold water. Serve with a dish of boiled potatoes.

### Carrot Charlotte

Take 8 ozs carrots, 4 ozs breadcrumbs, 1 oz suet, 1 orange rind or essence, 1 tablespoonful syrup, a few sultanas. Cook the carrots, diced or sliced, with orange rind or essence, syrup and sultanas in very little water, until water is absorbed. Mix the suet and breadcrumbs together and press part of the mixture into a greased pie dish. Add some of the carrots and repeat layers to fill the dish. Bake for about 40 minutes in a moderate oven. Turn out and serve with custard sauce.

### Braised Hare

Take a young hare, fat for larding, 2 carrots, a large turnip, 2 onions or leeks, 1 clove of garlic, parsley, rosemary, thyme, 1 bayleaf, salt and peppercorns – red wine if possible. Lard the hare well, highly season it. Slice vegetables in stewpan with herbs and cover with water and wine. Bring to the boil and simmer for half an hour. Add the hare and stew till tender. Take out the hare, strain the sauce, return the hare to the pan, pour the sauce over the hare and cook for a few more minutes. Carve the hare, cover with sauce, serve with potato balls and stewed currants."

VOGUE, February 1942

*Opposite* 'Mrs Henry Cavendish, the wife of Squadron-Leader Cavendish, does all the housework and cooking in her small house, a stone's throw from her husband's station. Her prize dishes are risotto and curry – as professional as her white chef's overall'
LEE MILLER 1942

# ALFRED LUNT COOKS FOR CHARITY
## by Elsa Maxwell

"At the Schlees' party Constance Collier pointed her forefinger at me as if it were a gun, and commanded me to join the Alfred Lunt Cooking Class for the benefit of the American Theatre Wing's Stage Door Canteen – at ten dollars for six lessons.

The first lesson was to be in one of the offices of the Theatre Wing at 735 Fifth Avenue. I arrived breathless, but beaming, as I always do at the prospect of *food*, in a small room on the twelfth floor, where were seated Lady Ribblesdale, with a pencil and pad, very lovely and earnest; Mrs William Randolph Hearst, senior, with a giggle and a pen. There were also Lady Mendl, busy collecting recipes (she wrote a cook-book herself); Mrs Somerset Maugham . . .

Then Amphitryon leaned out of his Olympian cloud in full chef's uniform, frying a slice of liver that seemed untouched by the high cost of living, and grilling a sole that defied comparison with Escoffier. 'Sole,' said Alfred softly, 'should never be brown – it should remain white when cooked.'

'Parsley is indispensable,' he went on. 'A woman might as well go out with a shiny nose as to allow a dish to appear from the kitchen without being powdered with parsley.'

He made another dish of baked creamed potatoes and eggs. 'You drop the eggs on the potatoes,' he said, 'and they come out of the oven like lovely little bridesmaids.'

He rambled on, 'We have three shelves of cook-books at home. One day I found the maid had put Somerset Maugham's *Cakes and Ale* amongst them. Good joke on Maugham,' he added, 'having to battle with Mrs Beeton.'

I asked Alfred, 'Is fat meat or lean meat the easiest to cook?'

'Lean,' said Alfred. Then he said, turning on me a speculative look, 'But Elsa, believe it or not, I could barbecue you so beautifully . . .' I took to my heels.

When he made spoonbread, I practically swooned, and snatching it from him, I consumed it all – smothered in butter . . . I, who live on Ry-Krisp.

So don't fail to join the class in the autumn, for you'll have to know how to cook as only Alfred Lunt can teach you – then I want him to cook a meal for the benefit of the American Theatre Wing at the Waldorf next autumn. Be sure to come – you'll not only eat wisely – but very well.

**Some of Mr. Lunt's most prized recipes:**
**Pot Roast**
3½ pounds of rump beef
2 tablespoonfuls of fat
1½ onions, chopped
½ tablespoonful of salt
3 anchovies
4 tablespoonfuls of vinegar
2 tablespoonfuls of syrup (or Karo)
16 peppercorns
16 allspice     2 bay leaves
2 cupfuls of stock (canned bouillon)

Cook everything together for about three hours, according to size of meat.

**Swedish Omelette (baked)**
4 eggs
1¼ cupfuls of scalded milk (cooled)
½ teaspoon of salt – pepper

Beat the eggs. Add milk, salt, and pepper. Heat a casserole. Grease with one tablespoonful of butter. Pour in mixture and bake fifteen to twenty minutes (400°F. oven).

VOGUE, June 1942

*Left* Alfred Lunt, actor and cook extraordinaire, teaches his cooking-class for the American Theatre Wing War Service
ERIC 1942

# COMMANDING FIGURES

"For four months, the Duke and Duchess of Windsor have been at Nassau, as Governor and Governor's Lady of the Bahamas. Their life now follows the steady, day-by-day routine of all British Colonial Governors and Governors' ladies. There are endless activities involved, some attended by a blare of publicity, others watched by no such barrage of cameras.

The Duke rises at 7.30, breakfasts at 8.30 and deals with his correspondence until 10, when he starts work in the Executive Office. Here he works until 1.15, when he and the Duchess have a light cold luncheon; the Duke has tea, which he brews himself. Afterwards, if no official function is scheduled, he returns to his office and works until 5. Then – if he is free – he plays golf and has a swim.

The Duchess works almost every day at the Red Cross Centre or the Dundas Civic Centre. (She plans to have the Red Cross meetings held at Government House, as soon as the alterations are completed.) The Duke and Duchess' leisure moments are generally spent in their garden, or shopping along Nassau's ancient Bay Street. But there are remarkably few leisure moments."

VOGUE, January 1941

"Lord Louis Mountbatten is the man of the hour . . . His every move is history, now. As Commander in Chief, South East Asia, he will be in supreme control over operations which he not only first

envisaged, but also perfected by long months of experiment, rebuff, innovation and rehearsal.

And Lady Louis? She too has met the challenge of reality with purpose and individuality. 'Just the wife of a Commando' is how she described herself, in a recent speech. Actually, she is something more. She is Superintendent in Chief of the Joint Red Cross and St John Organisation . . . Her day begins at 7 a.m. and often goes on till late in the evening . . .

She will switch her energies, after the war, to fighting for a better way of living, she says. She will expect, and want, to work just as hard. But *not* in uniform, please, she adds, with her quizzical, wry smile."

VOGUE, November 1943

*Above* The Duchess of Windsor, on her way to work at Red Cross Headquarters in Nassau, stops to look over plans for the renovation of Government House 1941

*Opposite* All in uniform: the Mountbatten family at Broadlands, their country house. BEATON 1943

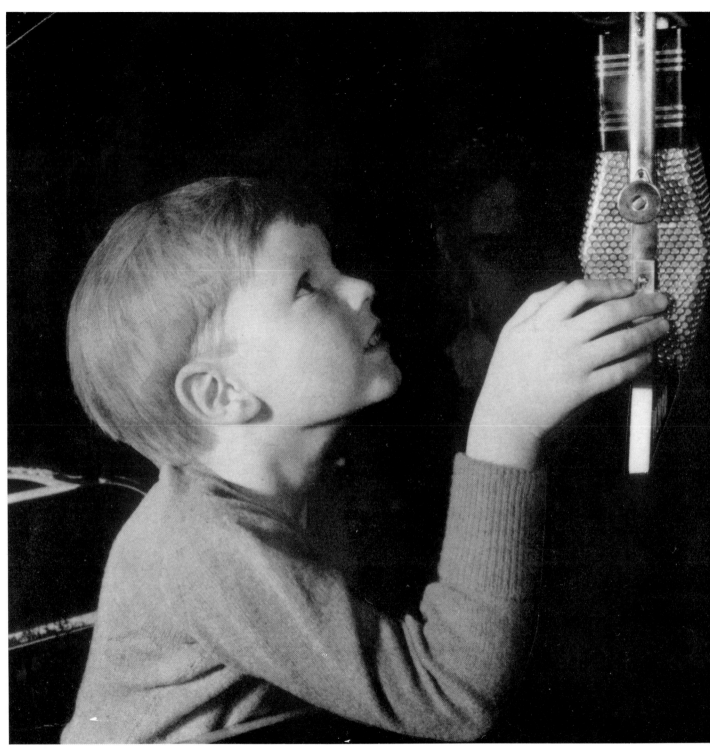

*Above, left to right*
Gawaine Baillie,
son of Sir
Gawaine and
Lady Baillie; David
and Niles Baird-
Murray; *centre*,
Bridget Caughey
TONI FRISSELL 1941

"Light and clear, out of the bright American afternoons into the loud darkness of Britain, go the voices of British children, broadcasting to their parents at home. Their small phrases of affection – the coin of every-day family life – are given a new and important significance.

Since September tenth, speaking every Tuesday afternoon at four, about a hundred and fifty children have taken part in this program, sponsored by the British-American Ambulance Corps, and called 'Friendship Bridge.' The voices go from WMCA's New York studios, and are re-broadcast, short

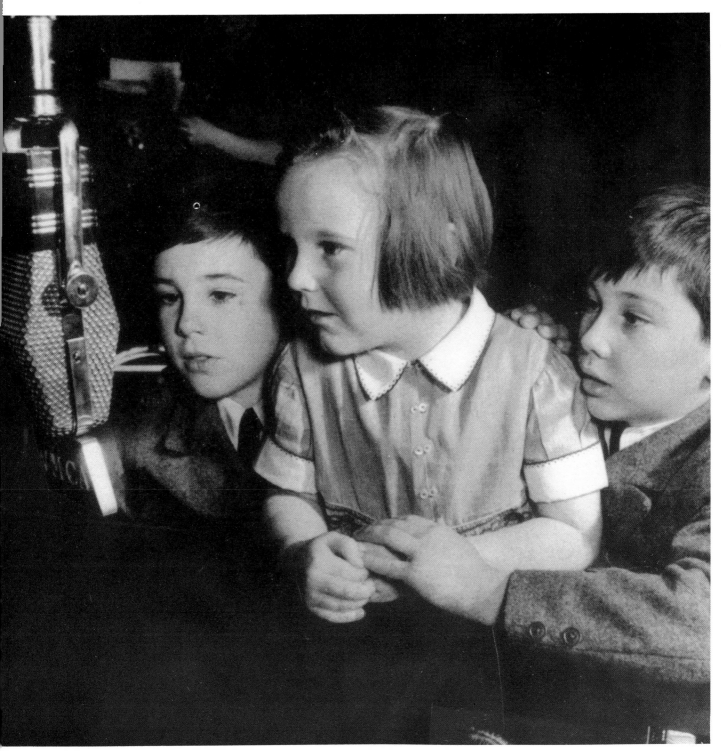

wave, from Boston's powerful WRUL.

The parents are notified by cable and can listen in on any short-wave set. They hear, usually, brief and dignified messages. Gawaine Baillie said only, 'Hello Mummy darling; hello Daddy darling,' but most children are more explicit. The Hodgkins, grandchildren of England's Lord Chief Justice Hewitt, said they had learned to swim and skate. (The most usual news.)

Their sturdy self-possession is touching – so is the fact that these human ties can now be sustained only by voices across three thousand miles.''

VOGUE, March 1941

# DEBUTANTES WITH A DIFFERENCE

"Last year débutantes curtsied to Royalty in fairy-story surroundings. This year they will not curtsey to Royalty at all; unless it be during the inspection of a branch of National Service.

Last year they lunched in each other's houses, dressed to the teeth. This year they have staggered snackbar lunches, dressed simply and suitably for canteen work or Red Cross classes.

Last year they wore nonsensical clips on their lapels. This year they wear regimental badges, or diamond wings.

Last year nanny and the maids gathered to admire their young lady in her court gown and feathers. This year they admire her brother in his uniform.

Last year, gardeners timed their prize blooms for the coming-out party of the daughter of the house. This year they timed prize vegetables for the coming-on-leave of the son of the house.

Last year mantelpieces were thick with formal invitations weeks in advance. This year telephone pads are thick with informal invitations rung through a few hours in advance.

Last year parties were planned; guests matched up, menus balanced. This year parties just happen; guests are whoever happens to be about; food is anything that isn't rationed.

Last year young men had to be decoyed to dances. This year, only service duties can keep them away.

Last year's favourite dances were Viennese waltzes and the 'Boomps-a-Daisy.' This year's favourite dances are Viennese waltzes and the 'Conga Chain.'

Last year the Derby was held, traditionally, at Epsom; Ascot at Ascot. This year both races are to be at Newbury.

Last year women were running households. This year they are running canteens, voluntary organisations, service units – and taking orders as well as giving them.

Last year time was no object: this week, next week, sometime . . . to dine, to dance, to meet, to marry. This year time is of the essence of the contract. Leave is reckoned in days, hours, minutes. Dates are timed to the split second and girls no longer keep boys waiting. 'Are you free next Wednesday – 4.30-8? I've special leave.' 'Can you lunch to-day?' 'Can you marry me to-morrow?'

Last year each event was written off as just another party. This year each event is chalked up as an achievement."

VOGUE, June 1940

*Above* Miss Mary Churchill, daughter of Britain's wartime Prime Minister
BEATON

*Opposite* Miss Pamela Tower, granddaughter of Mrs Harry Payne Whitney 'was to have made her debut this summer. Instead, she chose to give the cost of the party to her war charities'
TONI FRISSELL 1940

# Dancing in London

"Dancing in London. Many are the things that young people in London must do without. Safety. Security. Ease. But not dancing. They dance, in the photograph above, at the annual ball in aid of Queen Charlotte's Maternity Hospital. They dance in restaurants, at nightclubs. At the Mirabelle, during dinner. Later, at the 400 Club, where the lights are so low it's almost as dark as the blackout outside. They dance at the Savoy, in an underground shelter. They dance whenever they have an evening's leave.

They dance, seldom in evening dress – except at great charity balls like the

one that is photographed here. They dance in uniform: the men's – Army, Navy, RAF, or Allied; the girls' – ATS, WAAF. Girls on leave dance in bright wool day dresses.

They dance to the latest American jazz tunes; over and over, to their favourite, *Let There Be Love*. They dance all night – the restaurants close early, but the night-clubs stay open. Afterward, because of the taxi shortage, they often walk, cheerfully, home in the dawn."

VOGUE, December 1941

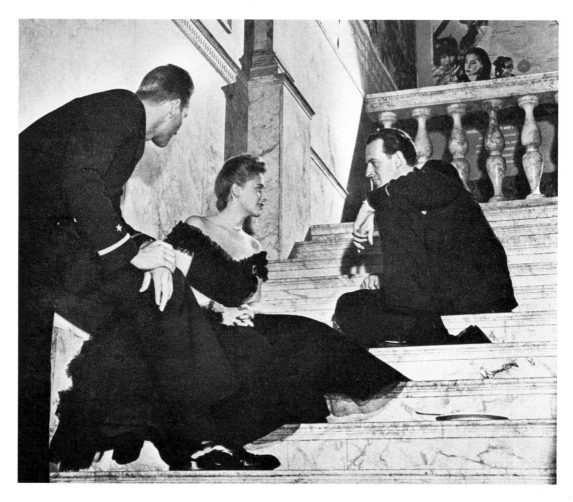

## ON LEAVE – NEW YORK ENTERTAINS

"Geography has made New York one of the great leave areas of this war – for enlisted men and officers, Army and Navy, American and Allied. To entertain them, there's a dance somewhere in New York every night in the week; most nights, there are several.

One of those held recently was the Junior Officers' Ball, given at the huge brownstone Whitelaw Reid mansion, by the Committee for American War Work of the Co-ordinating Council of French Relief Societies. Miss Rosemary Warburton, chairman of the Committee, received at the head of the marble staircase; the girls wore white gloves and their prettiest ball-dresses; and the party didn't break up till 4 a.m.

Then there are the regular Friday-night dances at the fabulous Open House for Officers, at Delmonico's. Started in August, it has entertained over 6,000 officers already. Officers drop in anytime between noon and midnight, to read, write, play bridge or backgammon or ping-pong, meet other officers, and meet girls – there's a carefully-checked list of 400 volunteer hostesses. On week nights, they dance to a juke-box that requires no nickels; on Friday nights, there's a formal dance. One of the few, but rigid, rules is that every girl must join in every Paul Jones – to prevent concentration. Even so, engagements are announced with astonishing frequency."

VOGUE, December 1943

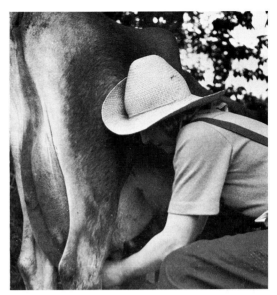

# LADY DIANA COOPER'S ONE-WOMAN FARM
## by Cecil Beaton

"Because Britain needs a bigger agricultural production, many a British woman has now turned farmer. Lady Diana Cooper, perhaps best known in America as the beautiful Madonna in 'The Miracle' is now best known in her own home village of Bognor as the able working-manager of a profitable farm. Many amateurs set about their latest hobby with expensive equipment, little knowledge, and no practice. Lady Diana, whose varied enthusiasms have been tackled always with a professional competency, has spent no more than fifty pounds, but a great deal of energy, perseverance, and ingenuity in her determination to 'produce more food.'

She keeps both chickens and ducks because their eggs replace the food values of 'fixed' price fish, of rare meat, and of canned foods. Lady Diana's cow, the dulcet Jersey 'Princess,' required a substantial outlay — twenty-eight pounds — but it keeps the family in milk, butter, and, what is more, in cheese.

The small house at Bognor is no Versailles Hameau. Rooms have been stored with stocks for farming; the erstwhile servants' hall is now the farm Still Room; the study is littered with dog-eared handbooks on Bee-keeping and the Poultry World.

No Marie Antoinette, Lady Diana buckles to hard work punctually for every appointment each day. The first date being for the milking of 'Princess' at 6.30 a.m. The morning is a rush to get through the various jobs after feeding the animals — collecting swill from neighbours and cheesemaking. In the afternoon there might be hay to be cut and brought back in sacks from an obliging neighbour's field — but whatever happens she is back for the feeding and milking before sunset.

Lady Diana Cooper, the outstanding Beauty of her generation and one of England's great Beauties of all time has, in a period perhaps poor in great characters, become ever more of a character — and with the years ever closer to essentials. In her latest phase she finds that, being fond of nature, there is no more agreeable pursuit than farming: added to the satisfaction of increasing the country's food supply."

VOGUE, September 1941

*Above right* Milking 'Princess', the Jersey cow
BEATON 1941

*Above left* Feeding the pigs
BEATON 1941

*Opposite* Tending the goat, in her working clothes topped off by sombrero and peasant scarf
BEATON 1941

# 'LIFE INSIDE THE FORT' – THE COUNTRY-HOUSE IN WARTIME

*Below* 'Big houses have been requisitioned; parks and gardens have been ploughed up.' Planting cabbages on the terrace of an ancestral hall, here, they 'dig for victory'
FRANCIS MARSHALL
1940

"Throughout Britain, many big houses are already converted into civilian hospitals, others being held in readiness, others again the temporary homes of evacuated children. There's a nice 'club' feeling about some country houses, where small groups of people have congregated – hostesses and guests each busy in the daytime with their various branches of National Service, returning every evening for a lovely interlude of normal, easy country-house life. As at Belton, where Lord and Lady Brownlow have friends with them who are working in the district; as at Kineton in Warwickshire, where Mrs Philip Dunne keeps open house for friends and their children."

VOGUE, September 1940

'Vaynol, Sir Michael Duff's house, the scene of many shooting parties and autumn holidays, is laid bare of its countless treasures. Pictures are put away, the mahogany doors taken off their hinges and the house transformed into an ideal hospital for soldiers. Every inch of his land is farmed. Land girls live in the outhouses. And he himself spends what little time he has on leave from the Merchant Navy directing the sawmills which hum more loudly than ever, turning out the much needed pit-props and planks; and consulting the farmer about the rotation of crops.

Lady Anglesey is very busy at Plas Newydd, the other side of the Straits, raising chickens, and telling evacuee mothers and children that potatoes don't grow wild! Lord Anglesey is out from dawn till dusk helping with the road defences and keeping his eyes skinned for suspicious craft hovering on

*Land cultivation: "Ancestral hall or no, the terrace must have more cabbages"*

the shores of the Straits. In other parts of Wales many women keep watch from castle turret tops – like Sister Anne, to see if anyone's coming.

Lady Howard de Walden had her large family of grandchildren at Chirk housed in her fourteenth-century fortress castle, but decided later that Canada would be even safer and took them all overseas. Her daughter-in-law, Mrs Scott-Ellis, divides her time between Chirk and her husband's station – somewhere in England.''

VOGUE, November 1939

*Left* Every inch of Sir Michael Duff's land is farmed'
1940

*Below* Evacuees from city bombing play on the safety of the lawn at Plas Newydd
RAWLINGS 1940

# PALM BEACH IN WARTIME – FLORIDA'S SEA-CHANGE

*Opposite* 'Bathing-suits in rolls, the SPARS go to the beach, singing.' SPARS were the women's reserve of the US Coastguards: their name derived from the motto, 'Semper Paratus', always prepared.
ALAJALOV 1944

*Below* 'The wheelchairs on Lovers Lane – pre-empted in olden days by the aged and infirm – are now engaged by sailors and their current inamoratas'
ALAJALOV 1944

"Florida, perhaps more than any of the States, has been transformed by the War. Miraculously, and almost over-night, its face has been lifted; not only as regards its superficial aspect, but its spirit, hardihood, and morale as well.

At Palm Beach, for example, the improbabilities are not only of a military, but social order. The Breakers, that extravagant and fashionable caravan-serai, has long been an Army hospital. The smooth and shining beaches, formerly the scenes of picnics and bathing parties, of happy trysts and soporific siestas, are now watched over by young Coast Guardsmen, either on horseback or patrolling on foot with their inevitable and terrifying police dogs.

Three of the larger hotels at Palm Beach are occupied by the military. The old Poinciana, long the best-known edifice in Florida, has vanished into thin air. Where it once stood, the SPARS – more than a thousand strong – now hold their elaborate parades and drills. These young and resolute ladies are headed, in their marchings and countermarchings, by an all-woman band, and commanded by women officers, all of whom – it has been ordained – must be addressed as 'Sir.'

Dinners at Palm Beach are all on the informal side, and rarely run to more than ten in number. Women of all ages dress almost as smartly, but far less pretentiously than they did. The wheel-chairs on Lovers' Lane – preempted, in olden days, by the aged and infirm – are now engaged by sailors and their current inamoratas. Where, formerly, fashionable young women dashed about in motor-cars, they now appear on motor scooters. Those of them who are engaged in patriotic duties think nothing of devoting ten hours a day to their jobs. Mrs Margaret Emerson, as an example, and her daughter, Mrs Baker Topping (with some help from their friends), feed and wait on three hundred Service men a day, at their popular 'V for Victory' canteen on the palm-lined Worth Avenue.

Most of the out-and-out Palm Beach night-clubs have either vanished or migrated to Miami. Swimming-pools are practically abandoned. Some of the better-known hostesses – Mrs Harrison Williams, for example – have opened only parts of their houses. Drinking has greatly abated, while gambling is principally indulged in by the migratory visitors from the North.

Despite all that has been said, there are still ways of diverting oneself at Palm Beach. Bowling, for example, has become a widely prevalent dementia. In place of yachts and motors, there are aquaplanes and bicycles. Mackerel and bluefish have had to pinch-hit for caviar and terrapin. People who once demanded a band now dance to a phonograph. As substitutes for long and late dinners, there are suppers and early movies. Gin rummy has, unbelievably, made serious inroads on bridge. The hotels are jammed. At the Everglades Club there are tombolas (modified lotteries), weekly fashion shows, and backgammon tournaments. Dancing – everywhere – ceases at twelve o'clock, the official hour of curfew, save for Saturday nights, when it falls at one-thirty.

What has added to the note of unreality in Florida's transformation is that, however grim in its details, it has been accomplished against so flowering and serene a background."

VOGUE, March 1944

*Bathing-suits in rolls,*
*the SPARS go to the beach, singing.*

# FIRST LADIES

"In Britain's greatest crisis, Mrs Churchill has taken her full share of the heavy job of organizing the defence and relief agencies of Britain. Like all British women, she has put aside her usual life – the brilliant dinners she used to give, all sports including her favourite skiing. But, though her days are full of duties, she still manages to look like a fine-boned, beautifully-dressed drawing-room ornament."

VOGUE, October 1940

"The Queen accompanies the King whenever possible, driving with him in the same carriage – dancing with him at Court Balls, and watching him at sport.

But as well as being his constant companion, she is also a practical and loving mother. She helps the Princesses with their lessons, often joins them in the terrifying snatch-and-grab game of Racing Demon, and takes a great interest in every detail of their education.

The King and Queen travel either in a shrapnel-proof car, or in the Royal train, which slows up but never stops during raids. The Royal coach serves as a palace on wheels, in which they sleep and have their meals. Their Majesties' suite is attractively furnished with armchairs in loose chintz covers, and such comfort as this is needed, as their journeys are often long and tedious.

*Right* Her Majesty Queen Elizabeth, with her husband King George VI, amid the bomb-damage at Buckingham Palace.
BEATON 1943

Everywhere people have wanted to known whether the Queen lost any of her belongings when Buckingham Palace was bombed. It was, in fact, her private sitting-room which suffered most, and several of her favourite things were shattered.

VOGUE, July 1943

"No President's wife has ever been more familiar to the citizens of America, or more widely beloved than she — newspaper columnist, radio commentator, and tireless philanthropist. Mrs Roosevelt has set her own precedents of unselfish benevolence, and broadened the position of a President's wife to fit her own spirit."

VOGUE, March 1941

*Above* Mrs Franklin D. Roosevelt, spirited wife of America's wartime President, dressed for the third Inaugural Ball
STEICHEN 1941

*Left* Mrs Winston Churchill, wife of Britain's Prime Minister, pours tea at No. 10 Downing Street
BEATON 1940

# CECIL BEATON AT WAR
## by Cecil Beaton

*Above* Cecil Beaton, in Transjordania, with members of Glubb Pasha's Arab Legion. After a decade-and-a-half as a brilliant chronicler of fashion and society, Beaton found a new depth and maturity during the war years, as an official photographer for Britain's Ministry of Information BEATON 1942

"Cairo, Teheran, Baghdad, Palmyra, Baalbec: these are some of the places I visited during the last three months. It sounds like some magic carpet tour, or pre-war millionaire's holiday. But no, I was sent by the Government to collect certain records and to take war photographs. During the trip I wrote notes in diary form . . .

**Tobruk** We pitched camp in a Wadi near the sea – almost an oasis, with fig trees, flowering cacti, wild flowers and wonderful birds. The gunfire like thunderstorms.

**El Hacheim** Don't mind dirt or discomfort. Am only sorry to leave forward areas . . .

**Iraq to Iran** Horrible mountains to fly over, especially when the heat pockets bang you about. At last we landed – Teheran. Rows of American bombers were lined up. The American white star to be painted red, then the aircraft are flown over by Russian pilots to Kuibishev.

**Transjordania** As the evening sun was sinking and casting long blue shadows on the desert scene, we came across another car. Colonel Glubb, in a khaki-coloured Tajrifa (headdress) was returning with a colonel and two highly-coloured henchmen from the camp a few miles on. Thanks to him, we had a thrilling evening being entertained by the Arab Legion in their scarlet, pink and khaki uniforms – sitting in a circle around a charcoal fire.

**En route for Home** We got into a flying boat . . . Silk-lined walls, arm chairs like Pullmans, compartments for eating, sleeping, smoking – this is the aircraft that took Churchill to America. How grateful I am to be among the lucky ones on the last lap for home."

VOGUE, October 1942

# CLARE BOOTHE LUCE AT WAR

"Clare Boothe, American journalist with a flair for front-page news, for being everywhere – Brussels . . . Paris . . . Amsterdam – just one step ahead of disaster, travelled in China with her husband, Henry Luce; visited the ancient city of Chung-king, which lies at the juncture of two circling rivers in the province of Szechwan; met the Generalissimo of the Chinese Army and Madame Chiang Kai-Shek.

The Luces were bewildered, at first, by Chung-king. It was difficult to distinguish between the masses of bomb-rubble and the battered, shack-like homes of the very poor, who swarm in every Chinese town. It was confusing to walk down wide, Western streets in which thousands of little Chinese shops of the traditional pattern stand next door to modern brick buildings smeared over with black paint; strange to ride sometimes in a high-powered motor-car, sometimes in a rickshaw drawn by coolies (who earn more than civil servants, these days) along these fantastic streets through which thousands of excitable Chinese people rushed continually.

In the first air-raids very many people were killed. Now the warning sounds well ahead of enemy 'planes, and the people of Chung-king know what to do. They 'just fold up their town, boarding up their shops, storing away their valuables and themselves into caves.' And the casualties are very small. The people are quite calm. As soon as the raid is over, they come out of their shelters and set their town in order. The theatres are open – theatres of every kind, plays of every kind – just as usual."

VOGUE, November 1941

*Left* Clare Boothe with Madame Chiang Kai-Shek, wife of the Chinese war-leader
S. C. CHUCK 1941

*Above* The beautiful Clare Boothe, wife of Henry R. Luce, publisher of *Time, Life* and *Fortune.* Author of three stage hits, including *The Women,* Clare Boothe became a renowned war-correspondent 1940

# PHOTOGRAPHIC SOURCES

AV indicates that the photograph or illustration was taken from an American edition of *Vogue*, BV and FV that it was from British or French editions. Although only one source is listed for each illustration, they may appear in more than one edition.

3  AV March 15, 1927
6  BV March 1942
8  AV Feb 15, 1948
9  BV Late Sept 1919
10  AV March 15, 1921 (top)
    BV late Jan, 1927 (bottom)
11  BV late Jan, 1927
12  AV Dec 1, 1924 (top)
    BV June 27, 1928 (bottom)
13  FV Dec 1937 (top)
    AV Dec 15, 1937 (bottom)
14  FV Aug 1934
15  BV Sept 28, 1932
16  AV July 15, 1929
17  AV June 22, 1921 (top)
    BV May 17, 1933 (bottom)
18  AV Sept 1, 1929
19  BV Sept 14, 1932 (top)
    FV Sept/Aug 1939 (bottom)
20  BV March 1940
21  BV April 1941
22  BV April 27, 1930
23  BV May 31, 1933
24  AV May 15, 1927
25  AV May 15, 1927 (top)
    AV May 15, 1927 (bottom)
26  AV Nov 10, 1930
27  AV Feb 15, 1927
28  BV May 29, 1935
29  FV May 1936
30  BV Jan 11, 1928
31  BV May 2, 1934
32  BV Jan 11, 1928 (drawing)
    AV July 15, 1932
33  AV Sept 15, 1930
34  BV Aug 8, 1928
35  BV Aug 8, 1928
36  BV March 6, 1935
38  BV Feb 15, 1928
39  BV April 29, 1936
40  AV Sept 1, 1930
41  AV Feb 15, 1931
42  AV Feb 15, 1931
43  AV Jan 1, 1922
44  AV Aug 15, 1939
45  AV Sept 1, 1932
46  BV May 2, 1937
47  AV Feb 1, 1933
48  AV Dec 15, 1935
49  AV July 5, 1930 (top)
    AV Feb 1, 1930 (bottom)
50  AV July 1, 1936 (main pic)
    AV Dec 15, 1924

51  AV Nov 15, 1938
52  BV Jan 23, 1935
53  AV March 15, 1933
54  FV July 1935
55  AV Dec 7, 1929 (top)
    AV Feb 1, 1937 (bottom)
56  BV May 1, 1929
57  BV March, 1928
58  AV Dec 15, 1937 (top left)
    AV Feb 15, 1931 (top right)
    AV Sept 1930 (below right)
59  BV Nov 30, 1927
60  AV Dec 15, 1937
61  AV Feb 1, 1930
62  BV May 1, 1929
63  AV Jan, 1936
64  BV Nov 15, 1935
65  BV July 15, 1938
66  FV Jan 1, 1926
67  AV Aug 1, 1936
68  FV Sept 1934
69  AV Jan 1, 1927
70  BV early Oct 1919
71  FV May 20, 1932
72  AV June 13, 1933
73  AV Nov 1, 1924 (top)
    AV March 15, 1927 (bottom)
74  AV March 2, 1929
75  AV March 2, 1929
76  BV Sept 28, 1932 (main pic)
    AV Oct 1, 1933
78  AV Sept 1, 1927
79  AV Sept 1, 1927
80  BV April 1, 1936
81  AV April 15, 1933
82  AV May 1934
83  AV March 1, 1927 (top)
    AV March 1, 1924 (centre)
    AV April, 1931 (bottom)
84  AV July 5, 1930
85  AV July 20, 1929
86  AV Nov 24, 1928 (top left)
    BV Sept 2, 1936 (top right)
87  AV March 15, 1933
88  BV May 1922
89  AV June 1, 1931
90  AV July 1, 1935
91  AV Oct 15, 1931
92  AV July 1, 1936
93  AV July 1, 1936
94  FV May 1929 (main pic)
    FV Jan 1, 1926
95  AV Aug 15, 1936 (main pic)
    FV Jan 1, 1926
96  BV Dec 14, 1938
97  AV May 1937
98  BV late April 1927 (top)
    AV July 16, 1929 (bottom)
99  AV May 1, 1937
100  BV March 6, 1935
101  FV March 1, 1926 (left)
    BV Jan 11, 1939 (top)

BV Dec 8, 1937 (bottom)
102  FV March 1, 1924
103  BV Dec 19, 1931
104-5  AV Dec 1, 1936
106  AV Aug 2, 1930 (main pic)
    BV Dec 11, 1929
107  AV March 29, 1930
108  BV early Jan 1922 (top)
    BV late March 1925 (bottom)
109  BV Nov 28, 1928
110  AV Oct 26, 1929
111  BV Sept 29, 1937
112  AV July 1935 (main pic)
    AV June 15, 1934 (insert)
113  BV June 27, 1934
114  AV Oct 1, 1931
115  AV Sept 15, 1920 (top)
    AV March 15, 1927
116  AV July, 1938 (main pic)
    BV Jan 11, 1928
117  BV late May, 1924 (main pic)
    BV Jan 11, 1928
119  AV Jan 15, 1933
120  FV May 1, 1929
121  BV late June, 1927
122  FV April 1, 1935
123  AV Sept 15, 1930
124  AV Dec 15, 1933
125  AV May 15, 1937
126  AV Aug 1, 1928
127  AV May 1, 1935 (top right)
    AV Sept 4, 1929 (top left)
    AV July 5, 1930 (bottom)
128  BV early Nov 1924
129  AV May 15, 1932
130  BV Sept 29, 1937
131  BV Aug 8, 1934
132  AV Nov 15, 1941
133  BV Aug 22, 1934
134  AV Aug 1, 1932
135  BV Sept 16, 1936
136  FV March 1, 1937
137  AV Nov 15, 1937
138  AV May 15, 1920
140  BV Oct 19, 1938
141  BV Sept 1, 1932
142  BV Feb 3, 1932 (top)
    BV Sept 20, 1933 (bottom)
143  BV May 30, 1934
144  AV Aug 14, 1928
145  AV Sept 15, 1932
146  BV late Aug 1923 (top)
    BV April 5, 1933 (bottom)
147  AV Jan 15, 1937
148  AV Oct 15, 1921
149  AV Aug 1, 1935 (top)
    BV Feb 22, 1928 (bottom)
150  AV Feb 1942
151  AV Aug 1942
152  BV Oct 1940

153  AV Feb 1942
154  AV Jan 1940
155  AV Jan 15, 1940
156  AV March 1, 1940
157  BV Jan 1940
158  BV Jan 1940
159  BV Jan 1941
160  AV Nov 1941
161  AV March 7, 1940
162  BV March 1941
163  AV March 1, 1942
164  BV Oct 1943
165  BV July 1942
167  BV Feb 1942
168  AV June 15, 1942
170  BV Nov 1943
171  AV Jan 1, 1941
172-3  AV March 1, 1941
174  AV Aug 15, 1940
175  AV Oct 1940
176-7  AV Dec 15, 1941
178  AV Nov 15, 1943
179  AV Dec 15, 1943
180  BV Sept, 1941
181  BV Sept, 1941
183  AV Sept, 1940
184  AV March 15, 1944
185  AV March 15, 1944
186  BV June 1945
187  BV Feb 1942 (top)
    AV Oct 15, 1940 (bottom)
188  BV Feb 1942
189  AV Nov 1941 (top)
    AV April 15, 1940 (bottom)

The colour illustrations appear opposite the page numbers listed below.
48  FV June 1937
49  AV Sept 1936
64  AV May 2, 1931
65  BV June 27, 1934
80  AV June 1, 1936
81  AV June 1, 1933
96  BV Jan 7, 1931
    AV Sept 1, 1937 (double page spread)
97  BV May 16, 1928
112  BV April 1933
113  FV Sept 1938
128  AV May 1, 1935 (top)
    BV Aug 21, 1929 (below left)
    BV May 17, 1933 (below right)
129  AV Feb 15, 1937
144  BV Jan 1, 1923
145  AV Oct 15, 1918 (top left)
    AV Aug 15, 1925 (top right)
    AV Aug 15, 1921 (below left)
    BV early July 1924 (below right)

# ACKNOWLEDGEMENTS

I should like to thank everyone who helped in the preparation of this book – in particular, Hilary Arnold, who brought the project into being, Cindy Richards, who edited the manuscript, and the designer Polly Dawes. The *Vogue* Library team, Fiona Shearer, Ingrid Nilsson and Merran Gunn, provided unstinting help; and the photographic knowledge of Robin Muir, *Vogue's* Picture Editor, was invaluable. Others to whom I owe special thanks include Lillie Davies of Condé Nast, and Barbara Bagnall at Random House. The extract from *Cold Comfort Farm*, by Stella Gibbons, is reproduced with permission from the author's estate.

The Cecil Beaton photographs on pages 33, 58 (top left), 132, 133, 141, 170, 180, 181 and 187 (bottom) have been reproduced by courtesy of Sotheby's London.

# INDEX